An EXPOSÉ on WING CHUN KUNG FU

THE GOLD SEAL OF LITERARY EXCELLENCE

Sifu Linda Baniecki

Order this book online at www.trafford.com
or email orders@trafford.com

Most Trafford titles are also available at major online book retailers.

Printed in the United States of America.

ISBN: 978-1-4669-0056-1 (sc)

Library of Congress Control Number: 2012900930

Trafford rev. 06/06/2012

 www.trafford.com

North America & international
toll-free: 1 888 232 4444 (USA & Canada)
phone: 250 383 6864 ♦ fax: 812 355 4082

AN EXPOSE' ON WING CHUN KUNG FU

By Linda Baniecki

An Expose' on Wing Chun

Kung Fu

Learn the intricacies of the concepts and principles in the Wing Chun Kung Fu system

DEDICATION

I would like to dedicate this book to my husband Garry Baniecki. For without his love, support and encouragement as a friend, Tong Moon (fellow Wing Chun exponent) and husband, my training my journeys and the writing of this book would never have been possible.

ACKNOWLEDGEMENT

I would like to thank the talented wing chun exponent Jesse Georgiadis, for helping me to show technique in this book. Also a big thank you to the Georgiadis family for their support throughout this project.

I would like to give a big thank you to Sifu Garry for his time, help and expertise on the photography in this book.

Table of Contents

About the Author

My maiden name is Linda Davis, (I am also known as Lil) I am 165cm and of slim build. I was born in 1956, in the border town of Albury in NSW, Australia. Although I have led a very active life, I had never considered doing Martial arts in my youth.

It would be fair to say, I have always been bit of a Tom boy.

I moved back to Melbourne from the country in July 1991 to be with my partner Garry Baniecki, whom I married and is now my beloved Husband.

Garry suggested that I might like to come along to a Kung Fu class that he had been attending. His plan was to become a teacher, so he was going to be spending a lot of his time there training.

In September of that same year Garry took me to Flinders St in Melbourne, to the William Cheung, Wing Chun Kung Fu Academy, to attend my first lesson where I trained under Sifu Dana Wong.

I loved it immediately and found that it occupied my mind constantly. I was forever going over techniques, and trying to make sense of the concepts in my mind, it was wonderful. I have not stopped my training and studies since that very first day 20 years ago. I began doing eight classes, fifteen hours a week which I maintained until I began teaching four years later. Having Garry there beside me was a great inspiration.

Within six months of training I joined the Demonstration Team and was also privileged to be invited by Sifu William Cheung to join his private class at the Dandenong Academy, for private tuition. Garry was also part of this small group.

Ten months later on our way to class Garry informed me that today we were not going to our usual class.

David Cheung (trained for 10 years under the infamous Wong Shung Leung, and 18 months under William Cheung his brother) had opened up his new Academy at 490 Elizabeth St, Melbourne and we were going to see if we could start training there.

I had heard a great deal about David and how he was a hard task master, I was nervous and I think Garry was too, even though he had trained with David for many years previously.

We were accepted as his students and trained lunch times at David Cheung's Academy and afternoons at the William Cheung Academy.

After a few months of training like this I made a decision to train with Sifu David full time instead of both Academies. He was a Master of Kung Fu; it was a new school with only a few students training there, which meant we were getting personal tuition everyday from a Chinese Master.

For me it was an easy decision. It was much harder for Garry as he had spent six years with William and was teaching the international class for him at the academy in the mornings.

However, the universe had a mission for the pair of us; it was our destiny to study under David, and in September 1992, 12 months after I began my training with William Cheung, Garry and I both started training full time with Sifu William's brother, Sifu David Cheung.

The school became involved in Chinese Lion Dancing and each year I would train hard to earn my place in the head of the lion. We performed for many weeks around Melbourne during the Chinese New Year festival. This caused a bit of controversy at the time as the head of a lion was traditionally a man's job.

The old saying goes that when the student is ready the Teacher will come.

In 1993 Dr Shan Hui Xu (pronounced Sui) Qi-Gong Master from China and trained at the Shaolin Temple entered our training hall, he could not speak a word of English. (Studied under the world's leading Qi gong Masters Hot Guen Tong and Ling Kwok and was Vice President of the Ma Wang Dui Qi gong Training Centre)

His lack of English did not deter us and within a couple of months we had begun our introduction to Qi Gong training with Dr Xu. After twelve months Garry and I could understand Dr Xu better than anyone else, and we began lecturing for him in his classes. We spent the next eight years studying and demonstrating Medical Qi Gong and Iron Shirt Qi Gong privately under this Qigong master whilst training WC under Sifu David Cheung.

This training enhanced our psychology and the way we thought of our health, our life and Wing Chun.

It was through this training that we introduced new breathing techniques into our Wing Chun teaching, as well as other Shaolin tools for strengthening and building the Qi, rather than just relying on the Sil Lim Tao form. This made our school a bit of a talking point around Melbourne and Australia in the Wing Chun fraternity.

In 1994 I entered my first competition, the Australian Full Contact Kung Fu Championships which was held at the WMCA Elizabeth St Melbourne; there were only three girls, we did a round robin and I placed 2nd which I was extremely proud of at the time, as it was my first battle in combat and I was 38 years old.

Enjoying the buzz of competing but realizing that I was a bit mature for full contact, in 1995 I entered the non contact National All Styles competition with sparring and forms. This was predominantly a Karate competition at the time, with a little bit of bias toward Kung Fu systems. This just meant I would have to work much harder to have them respect our system.

Competing in the black belt division changed the way I trained my forms forever, I realized I needed to place more emphasis on breathing, speed, power and definition. I trained this new formula with great intention to eventually become the National All Styles Victorian Open Black Belt Forms Champion and Open Black Belt Synchronized forms Champion in 1997.

In 1995 myself and Garry, commenced 12 months instruction of unarmed combat: empty hands self defense skills, disarming techniques (against rifles and bayonets), and the deadly art of Traditional Wing Chun Kung Fu to the Australian Army's School of Signals and the 123 Single Squadron Commandos, at the Watsonia Army Barracks. Melbourne Victoria.

In December 1995 I was graduated to Sifu, by Master David Cheung, and in 1996 I began teaching children and adults at our (Garry and myself) academy at 24 Lorimer St Greensborough Vic which Garry opened in 1994.

The school is active to this day.

In 1996 I joined the NAS committee and became a referee and judge where I met a lot of people from different denominations and learnt a great deal about competition and competing.

In 1997 David left Melbourne and Garry and I took over the teaching and running of the Elizabeth St School, which has since been relocated to 96a Hoddle St, Abbotsford in Melbourne.

In 1998 we travelled to Sydney with a group of students to compete in the ISKA (International sports karate association) World Cup Championships. Even though we had no winners it was a wonderful experience meeting people from all over the world and competing on such a large scale. There were 80 competitors in the men's open Black Belt Division.

In 2001 I competed in the Australian Kung Fu Championships where I placed 2nd in the Open Weapons Division with Traditional Wing Chun Dragon pole form.

In 2004 I became the Victorian Veterans Open Black Belt Sparring Champion.

From between 1995 and 2004 I qualified for the Victorian Team and traveled to Western Australia, Sydney and Queensland to referee, judge and compete.

I still love to compete with weapons and non contact sparring when the opportunity arises.

In 2005 we became involved in full contact Muay Thai where we have developed quite a few good fighters using wing chun principles and concepts. This is still an ongoing venture. One of our dreams is to one day train a Wing Chun practitioner to Champion status in Muay Thai or MMA.

Through the influence of our three teachers, our own intellect, having a good understanding of the concepts and theories of the Traditional Wing Chun system and Qi Gong, Garry and I have nurtured and developed Jee Shin Wing Chun into a unique and dynamic Martial Art.

Through our patience, dedication, diligence and love for the art, we now live our dream and our life is filled with the teaching of Wing Chun Kung Fu, Qi Gong, and Tai Chi.

It is a perfect career choice that I would recommend for everyone.

Many people are lucky enough to be trained by one Master; to have trained under three Masters was beyond my expectations or belief.

I believe in destiny and that the universe placed Garry and I in the path of these people, to teach us great knowledge, and give us an opportunity to pass it on to the rest of the world through our passion. Which we are endeavoring to do through the different courses we offer in and around Melbourne as well as from our Schools in Greensborough and Abbotsford.

I began the idea of writing this book in 2006, and have since managed to travel to China four times. Meeting and demonstrating with many different Masters and training under yet another Master, Fung Keun of Kulo. What a wonderful experience that was.

Garry and I have spent many hours talking with his father, 90 years young Master Fung Chun, which has always been a real honor.

These journeys and talks can be viewed on You Tube.

Talking with Fung Chun has also reconfirmed my personal belief in the history of Yim Wing Chun as the inheritor and major developer of the Wing Chun system.

My journeys in Kung Fu have been an amazing adventure and is far from over. I still have many more experiences to have, people to meet, and knowledge to learn. When I began my path in Wing Chun I never dreamed the path would stretch so far, my life is truly blessed.

Introduction

Wing Chun Kung Fu is truly one of the genuine secrets and treasures of the Shaolin Temple. This art was devised during a time of upheaval and revolution and developed through a period of strife and chaos. Its sole purpose was to kill the enemy, "Destroy the Qing and return the Ming"; making it a truly unique Martial Art.

The creators of this system were the Shaolin monks, Ming Generals, Kung fu and Qigong experts, and Rebels.

The northern and southern temples were the places where the idea of Wing Chun started. The monks had to develop a fighting strategy to learn quickly, with a focus on economy of movement and the science of bio mechanics, to enable the Chinese to destroy their enemy.

It is steeped in Buddhist and Taoist philosophy and the principles of Yin and Yang.

For the system to include Dim Mak, pressure point attacks, it would be imperative for the practitioner to have a very good understanding of the Chinese energy system.

Wing Chun Kung Fu's core principles are; central line theory and center line theory. This incorporates, straight line attack, economy of movement, simultaneous and independent movement of arms and legs, trapping and controlling, Qi development, Dim Mak pressure point attacking, focusing on the elbows and the center of gravity. Not fighting force on force: mobility, interrupt ability, balance and circular footwork.

Its strength is built around the science of the human body, and the understanding of energy, space and time, not on animal movements. The art of fighting may change, but the human body and the science of energy, space and time stay the same.

Eye reflexes and contact reflexes are trained and heightened through specific drills, referred to as Qi Sao, raising ones sensitivity levels and reaction time. The hand is quicker than the eyes; this is why we have such great Magicians in the world, and a good reason why we can't afford to rely on watching the hands or the fists in combat.

The wooden man, "Muk Yan Jong" is an essential part of Wing Chun and the system cannot be taught correctly without the use of this ingenious tool.

All ranges of combat are covered as well as non-contact and retreat.

Traditional Weapons include the Bart Jarm Dao (Butterfly Swords) for close range combat and the Kuan (Dragon Pole) for long range fighting.

All these aspects put together, make Wing Chun one of the greatest over all fighting system's in the world.

National Geographic covered a documentary on histories most deadly weapons and wing chun was classified in this documentary as the most deadliest empty hand weapon in history.

Now through the movies that are being produced on Yip Man, the grandmaster of wing chun, and his history, Wing Chun is set to rise to even greater heights as a whole new generation of people discovers the beauty of the Wing Chun system.

Preface

Wing Chun is a very popular martial art around the world, especially in China, its concepts and principles remain the same wherever the art is taught and practiced.

However the way in that one person imparts their knowledge, compared to another can be quite different. Wing Chun is a conceptual art, and how a person perceives the information, will depend on how they will teach or pass on their information.

This makes Wing Chun a very versatile art, as everyone sees things in their own way, even when sticking to the same principles and concepts.

This book was written on the basis of the Jee Shin Wing Chun's concepts and principles of the art. Some systems may not use all of the principles and concepts used in the Jee Shin System of Wing Chun and some systems may have other concepts and principles, or even other ideas on the concepts and principles used in this book.

This is the versatility of Wing Chun.

My passion for this great art was my inspiration for writing this expose'.

This is my interpretation, of my understanding of the system and I hope all who read it find it stimulating and rewarding and that it may encourage many more people, especially women to take up this wonderful martial art.

Chapter One

The Sil Lim Tao Form

We will begin our journey into this mysterious system of Wing Chun with the first of the four forms, Sil Lim Tao, translated as 'The Shaolin Way' or 'Little Idea Form'.

Sil Lim Tao is the first open-hand form in the Wing Chun system. The form may also be called Sil Nim Tao or Sil Lum Tao.

Sil Lim Tao is also a form of moving and breathing meditation. In addition, it increases student concentration and focus on the whole body.

When a person observes someone practicing Sil Lim Tao, it truly looks as though it is a very basic form with not much to offer in the way of development or ideas, maybe this is why they gave it the name Little Idea Form.

This could not be further from the truth. Hidden within this humble form are all the elements to begin the development of the whole body in a very unique way, as well as training all the basic theories, principles, concepts and techniques of the Wing Chun system.

All great achievements start from a small idea.

The concepts and principles that are trained in this form include central line theory, centre line theory, economy of movement, focus, forward intention, independent movement of the limbs, perception of distance in relation to our opponent, and an introduction to simultaneous movement of arms and legs.

The training of Sil Lim Tao also aids in developing other principles of the art, which include internal Chi development and flow, correct breathing, balance, coordination of the mind and body, posture, stamina, concentration and focus, independent and simultaneous movement of the limbs, 50/50 weight distribution, flexibility of the arms and wrists, the training of each individual hand technique, the neutral stance and side neutral stance.

The correct knowledge of Wing Chun follows the theory of the science of the human body and the science of energy, (Bio mechanics and the laws of physics), one must understand this technical knowledge to fully comprehend the Wing Chun system. The practitioners mind and body really need to come together, coordinate themselves and become one, for this empty hand system to become one's own.

Whilst training the Sil Lim Tao the mind must continuously and consciously guide and direct ones intention and energy (Qi) over the entire body, teaching it how to conserve energy by minimizing movements for efficiency in hand to hand combat.

Wing Chun does this through the repetition of movements; therefore a practitioner needs to be patient and willing to dedicate oneself to the time it takes to understand the basics of this art; for they are the foundation for the higher training skills. This means training the Sil Lim Tao over and over again, along with other basic training drills.

As the great Musashi said, "when you practice something, the more you practice the same thing, the spirit of the thing will become comfortable with you. When it becomes comfortable with you, the spirit of the thing will reveal itself to you and take you to another level of understanding."

This saying is absolute in Wing Chun. By correctly applying oneself to the repetition of Sil Lim Tao (and all other basics) the practitioner should start to understand the core of the science and the deepness of what the form is really trying to express to the practitioner . . . . . . some people never get it and their wing chun remains just aerobic movement.

One is drilled into the correct positions of body movements, correct range, accumulation and direction of energy and intention through the repetition of the Sil Lim Tao form.

When one begins training, students have little knowledge on the perception of distance, which we refer to as range or space. Individuals do not know the length of their own arms and legs, where the top of their head is, or what the distance or space is from their opponent, the training of the Sil Lim Tao teaches us all this and more, through the continual repetition of this form.

The Sil Lim Tao form can be likened to your ABC, first you need to learn the basic letters before being able to read or write a single word. Once one begins to understand their ABC they can then progress onto writing and reading simple sentences, then advancing even further to paragraphs, pages and eventually being able to express themselves by writing a whole book.

The same applies in Wing Chun Kung Fu, one starts off very basic and through repetition ones knowledge slowly progresses until eventually a very high skill level is reached when reaction becomes reflex.

Sil Lim Tao trains and develops; both sides of the body equally, keeping the left and right sides of the body symmetrically balanced, including the brain.

Initiating both hemispheres of the brain at once, not only challenges the mind and body, but stimulates an incredible amount of hormones into the human body, which uplifts the immune system and keeps the body in tremendously good health.

Assuming the majority of humans are right handed, all movements begin on the left, followed by the right side; thus enabling both sides of the body to be trained equally.

To begin practicing the Sil Lim Tao Form one begins by centering one's mind, body and breath before opening up into the Neutral Stance.

As in Traditional Shaolin Styles, the arms are raised and stretched out to shoulder height; the hands are made into fists (photo 1) and retracted back to the sides of the body at chest height (photo 2).

1) SLT preparation   2) fists retracted

In the Wing Chun system the arms are retracted back to chest height, kept just off the body, held parallel to the ground and the body. This stimulates the brain to be continuously aware of the arms, whilst in a static position; this is the first stage of being able to control both arms independently from each other and the body.

3) Neutral stance

The practitioner then bends the knees, lowering the center of gravity and stabilizing the body.

The left foot is picked up, circled out to the left side landing toe first with the heel turned slightly out (refer to Sil Lim Tao photo 3).

The right foot is then circled out to the right side, landing on the ball of the foot first.

The left foot is adjusted in, so the feet are shoulder width apart, weight distributed evenly between the feet with the toes slightly pointed in on a 45 degree angle (photo 3). Adjusting the left foot last, trains the concept of always adjusting both feet when mobile, enabling the practitioner to keep their stance shoulder width apart, and their balance fifty—fifty over both feet.

The arms must be controlled and remain in their position while the lower body is initiated. Control the whole body.

The toes grip the floor, (connecting Kidney 1 point to the earth and stimulating and strengthening the Spleen, Stomach, Bladder, Gall Bladder and Liver meridians) with the feet placed 45 degrees to the front, giving one a slightly pigeon toed appearance, creating a triangular base; being one of the strongest and most stable bases for a vertical structure (photo 3).

The chin should be tucked in and the tongue placed on the roof of the mouth, acting like a circuit breaker to join the front (Wren) and back (Du) Vessels together. This allows for the correct flow of Qi around the body, called the Macro Cosmic Orbit (photo 4).

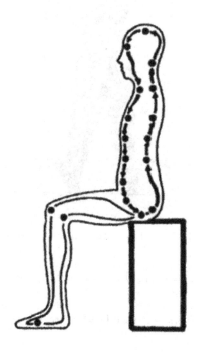

4) Macro Cosmic orbit

Shoulders are pulled back and the coccyx is tucked in slightly to align the spine, Pak Wei on the crown of the head, is aligned to the universe for the absorption of Yang energy while the Hui Yin in between the legs is aligned with the Earth for the absorption of Yin energy. Training the correct breathing and alignment of the posture will open meridians, encourage the correct energy flow around the body, aid in the production and development of Qi.

Standing in the correct posture Training Sil Lim Tao for lengths of time also train ones stamina in the arms and legs. It is very common to see beginners become faint due to jelly legs during the form. This is due to lack of circulation in the upper and lower gates of the body. Continual practice will improve blood and Qi circulation, creating a smoother flow of blood and Qi within the whole of the internal body, improving one's health immediately.

When an individual begins Qigong training, (internal development training) the student usually starts by meditating on only two points, which is usually the breath and posture.

In The Jee Shin Wing Chun Kung Fu system, the beginner learns to meditate on eight points simultaneously in the Sil Lim Tao Form, expanding one's mind, uplifting ones focus and concentration. This produces an extremely elevated meditation for Qi cultivation and over all body development, eight being synonymous with the Chinese Ba Qua (photo 5).

5) Later Heaven Ba Qua Symbol

The eight points are;

- Toes continually gripping the floor.

- Knees bent to drop the centre of gravity down.

- Tailbone tucked in to align the back with the anus lightly contracted.

- Shoulders back, fists pulled back at chest height, off the body, parallel to the body and the ground.

- Chin tucked in to align the crown of the head with the universe.

- Tongue on the roof of the mouth, for the circulation of Qi—energy around the micro cosmic orbit.

- Independent movement of both the arms. (Forward intention with the moving hand, whilst keeping the parallel arm static.)

- Breathing.

When the practitioner can apply his mind to the whole body and keep all these points alive with energy and functioning correctly, then he/she is on their way to understanding the hidden secrets within the Sil Lim Tao form and mastering the Wing Chun system.

Balance

The Wing Chun practitioner is trained to be balanced at all times during combat and the training for this begins with the Sil Lim Tao Form.

The formula for **power**; is balance + speed = power.

The concept of always keeping the weight distribution fifty—fifty over each foot, allows for the body to stay balanced, which maximizes the formula for power.

When a practitioner can keep evenly balanced with footwork, it frees the brain to allow for 100% focus on all weapons in both the upper and lower gates for combat. Being balanced also stops a person from leaning and over committing. The Jee Shin Wing Chun system will step in to make the distance to the opponent, or away from the opponent, never leaning or over committing. This allows the WC practitioner to interrupt his/her movement at any given time, whilst taking advantage of the formula for power.

Once a person over commits and leans, they become slow and their ability to be dynamic with footwork and technique is eliminated. The fighter must keep transferring the weight to enable him to pick his feet up, expending energy and brain power, slowing him or her down tremendously and ultimately taking his power away. This is when people rely on force and luck in combat.

Balance is imperative if you want to float like a butterfly and sting like a bee (Mohamed Ali).

Understanding how important balance is to our own prowess, the Wing Chun practitioner will use this against their opponent by attacking, controlling and disrupting the Opponent's balance physically and mentally with every available opportunity. Giving the Wing Chun practitioner split seconds in time to take advantage of the weakness they have created in the opponent's defenses.

Being balanced allows for explosive, dynamic footwork, for entering or relocating on the opponent during combat.

This training in balance extends even further to include the physical body being trained symmetrically. Both left and right sides are trained equally, in both the upper and lower gates, keeping the physical body balanced. This helps to create a very healthy internal environment, also enabling the practitioner to be comfortable using either the left or right side in combat or life.

The practitioner is trained to access both spheres of the brain simultaneously enabling the use of the left and right sides of the body to be used equally, in doing so releasing large amounts of life giving hormones for health and longevity.

Wing Chun training offers great health and spiritual benefits to all who practice, making it an excellent exercise for the average person who would like to uplift there health, stay in shape, tone up, challenge the mind and stay strong and healthy throughout life. Think of it as basic exercise with a difference.

Learning how to protect yourself and your family in aggressive situations with this practical system is an added bonus.

The Central Line Theory

Jee Shin Wing Chun is based on the central line system.

The central line theory is one of Jee Shin Wing Chun's unique major principles.

Our theories, concepts and principles are concentrated within the central line area.

This is an imaginary box like area in front of the body that covers the upper, middle and lower gates. This area is designated in Sil Lim Tao where a practitioner can cross both wrists in the upper, middle and lower gates, without pivoting the body (photo 6). Inside these six gates all attacks and defenses will take place.

Keeping within this box or area will ensure that the practitioner does not over commit, use excessive energy or lean, giving him economy of movement within this area, as well as the ability to utilize both hands and legs at the same time for attack and defense, in the upper, middle and lower gates.

Central line gives the Wing Chun practitioner a Centre line and an outer gate line.

6) Central line lower gate

6) Central line upper gate

For example all single arm attacks will utilize central line theory and take the centre line path, whilst the outer gate will be protected with the free hand (photo 7).

7) Central line application

In application if the practitioner turned at the waist the Central Line area would move with him in front of his body.

It is through the science of the central line theory that a Wing Chun practitioner is able to use arms and legs simultaneously in the six gates of the central line, giving him a great advantage over his opponent.

Self defense is like dancing, it relies on rhythm and timing to a beat, for it to be effective.

In self defense, when one uses simultaneous attacks and defense to a rhythm, the beat becomes a one rhythm—block and attack together, rather than a one and two rhythm of block and then attack.

We will discuss the Central Line more in the next topic.

Centre Line Theory

The centre line differs from the central line. This is an imaginary line of symmetry dividing the body vertically in two halves.

The centre line is used as a line of sight for linear attacks in combat, giving us the shortest path to our opponent.

All traditional multiple chain punches will be applied along the centre line path, just inside the lead leg, using centre line theory.

All major organs (photo 8) are on or very close to the conception (Wren) vessel (the centre line of the body), and major vital pressure points relating to the body and organs lay along the Conception vessel or center line, which is the major Qi Vessel on the front centre line of the torso.

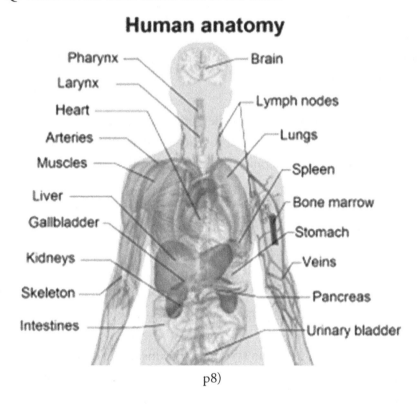

p8)

The Conception Vessel or centre line starts at the Hui Yin in between the legs, (situated in front of the anus) runs up the front of the body past the belly button, sternum, chest, throat and finishes under the tongue on the bottom jaw. (see diagram 4)

Striking along this path can cause serious if not detrimental internal damage to your opponent, even death.

In defense the goal in Wing Chun is to cover and guard the centre line, guarding and protecting these vital pressure points and making it impossible for the opponent to come through the centre unless we choose to let him enter. Guarding or controlling the centre will make the opponent take the longer circular path, around your lead arm to attack, allowing the WC practitioner to use the concept of the straight line attack (straight punch) through the centre, the shortest distance between two paths.

Whilst, **when in attack mode**, the goal in wing chun is to attack and control the opponents centre line. When there is an obstacle (opponents guard, arm, punch) blocking the centre line, chi sao, feigns and redirections are used to create openings and find the path with the least resistance, along the centre line to the opponent.

The system uses the straight line principle with kicks and punches; punches are vertical, in both multiple and single, and the back fist can be used, utilizing the straightest path from the point of contact; circles are only used for the redirection of forces, disruption of the opponents balance, coverage of the upper and lower gates and the releasing of grabs.

There are no actual blocks to stop punches in Wing Chun, only deflections. Wing Chun deflects and redirects forces rather than applying a block to stop the punch or force. Applying this method of 'stopping the force' is referred to as fighting force against force. The WC practitioner never fights force against force, instead they will let the force go in its natural direction and take advantage of the openings that have been offered through the commitment of the opponent.

It is through the use of the centre line that enables the wing chun practitioner to utilize the **science of the Central line theory**. This science enables the fighter to utilize two arms at the same time; allowing for attack and defense simultaneously through specific positioning of the body.

To develop this ability one must become adept with the Sil Lim Tao Form and then Chum Kieu Form. These forms train the mind to control arms, legs and the whole body to function and come together as a complete unit.

Sil Lim Tao trains in the development of, focus, centre line theory, stance, and two arms to be independent of one another, cultivates Chi and gives us a perspective of range, plus much more.

Chum Kieu is the third form in the Wing Chun system and trains in the development of central line theory, develops the whole body to work as a complete unit, trains both arms and legs to work independently and simultaneous of each other and of the body itself, develops footwork, kicking, speed, balance and positioning.

In systems, where brute force is used, body momentum and over commitment are employed, rather than using the science of speed, positioning, interrupt ability and balance. Central line is one of the hardest theories to grasp in the Wing Chun system.

Jee Shin Wing Chun is a Central line, trapping and controlling system that utilizes Centre line theory, which is contained within the Central line.

The central line box does not only contain the one true centre line, but is made up of many centre lines.

(photo 9) This science is one of the hardest concepts for a practitioner to grasp and master, but is a must for understanding the JSWC system.

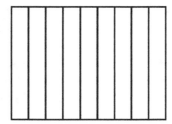

9) The many lines inside the Central line box

For successful application of the central line theory, the practitioner must use the centre line (one of the lines in the box) as a point of reference for the deflecting arm. The centre line on the body, faces the point of contact on the deflecting arm (point of contact—where your arm touches the opponents arm or leg to deflect the attack) this enables the practitioner to attack and defend simultaneously in the upper or lower gates (photo 10). Giving the Central Line Wing Chun exponent incredible attacking speed and the opportunity to create and take advantage of many more windows of opportunity during combat.

During altercations, being able to take advantage of these windows of opportunity can make the difference between winning and losing.

10) Simultaneous attack and defense   11) Upper and lower gate defense

11) Upper and lower gate defense   12) Defense and attack

The centre line must always face the point of contact, within the central line, and if you dropped a string line from the point of contact to the ground, the lead foot would be directly beneath this point.

Incorporating two arms for defense only, allows for the coverage of the upper and lower gates simultaneously, (photo 11) the centre line must be used as the point of reference and be facing the point of contact to allow for this to happen. Once this position has been initiated, the practitioner is in the correct (photo 12) position, to apply the use of leg attacks simultaneously whilst using the arms to defend.

Therefore utilizing both arms in the central line for defense also gives us the ability to attack simultaneously with not only the arms but also the legs.

Simultaneous attack and defense is very effective in breaking your opponent's rhythm and timing during combat.

Using two arms to protect the upper and lower gates when you are not sure of where attacks are coming from, or when your vision has been impaired, (drink or sand thrown in your face, blood in your eyes, it's too dark) gives you coverage of the whole body, enabling you to cover and find contact with the attack where ever it might come from.

Once contact has been found, you are able to deal with the attack from the opponent, through your understanding of the human body; Qi sao and the science of wing chun, if these situations arise.

Wing Chun Guard

p13

The JS Wing Chun system stresses that you must be able to see, to defend, if you block your vision and cannot see the attacks, then you have lost your advantage and are more likely to be hit, injured and lose the fight.

Wing chun does not just rely on the eyes; the hands are quicker than the eyes, this is why we have such great magicians in the world.

Wing Chun relies on sensitivity and the feeling of which direction the forces are taking.

The basic JSWC guard has the lead arm stretched out along the centre line (photo 13) with the wrist cocked, elbow slightly out, bottom knuckle of the thumb in line with the nose, thumb tucked in with fingers packed together facing forward toward the opponent.

The elbow is slightly out to allow for a full visual under the wing chun guard, at the **opponents elbows** which anatomically lay at the centre of gravity, enabling the WC practitioner to see at all times the path where the attacks will be emanating from. If we can see, we can win.

Taking this position will make it impossible for the opponent to punch straight through the centre, his only option is to take the longer circular path, around the guarding arm, or come below the lead arm. Thus giving the wing chun practitioner's lead arm the straight line attack either way.

This lead guard protects the head which contains the most important organ in the body, the brain. It also utilizes the length of the arm to keep the opponent at a safe distance. This basic lead guard uses centre line theory and is only used in defense. What type of guard you have is not really important.

The practitioner must always be aware that the lead arm can be grabbed when stretched out in front to defend, so observing the elbows at this time is very important.

The rear guard (see photo 13) arm is parallel to the floor across the body, half way between the upper and lower gates, the wrist is cocked with the tips of the fingers sitting just below the top of the bicep. This allows for minimum movement to defend the upper and lower gates with the rear arm.

This type of guard is strictly used for defense only, one would not bridge the gap and attack with this basic guard. Other strategies would be used, depending on the situation and the opponents stance and guard.

The Wing Chun system is a thinking man's system, it is not just devised on aerobic movements. When the Wing Chun practitioner decides to move in and attack, the situation must be assessed and you must decide what strategy will be used, that would allow you to get from A to B successfully.

Because this system masters movement and fighting skill through repetition, the wing chun practitioner does not really think about what to do, he just instinctively knows the best strategy to use through observing where the openings are or are not and what type of guard the opponent has. This instinct comes through sheer repetition in training.

If there are no openings, then one must be created through the use of strategy, then Qi sao.

If the Wing Chun practitioner uses a strategy that removes his lead guard from the upper gate whilst moving forward for an attack or feign, the rear guard can be raised to protect the head.

The rear guard would be raised on the outer gate, while the lead arm would cover the centre line path, this utilizes central line theory (photo 14).

14) Utilizing central line   14a) Pinning a kick

Wrist flexibility

The wrists are flexed with rotations and in Fuk Sao during the training of the Sil Lim Tao Form. It is very important to keep full range of motion in the wrists for flexibility not only for combat but for general life.

Flexing the wrist also aids in the stretching and strengthening of the meridians, muscles, tendons and ligaments in the wrist, forearms and the actual joint. A flexible strong wrist is needed to support the fists when punching, to apply Lop Sao (grabbing hand) for control and manipulation of the opponent. Also to support Biu Gee strikes into a target (thrusting fingers strike) and the deflection of the reactionary force that will come through the fingers from the strike and reverberate out the wrist.

Without a strong flexible wrist all the reactionary force from the strike would reverberate into the fingers causing damage.

Training full motion enhances ones range of flexibility in this area for the use of tight, fast circular (Huen sao) movements to redirect forces.

Flexible strong wrists are also needed for the use and application of the Kwan (Dragon pole) and the Bart Jarm Dao (Eight Slash Butterfly Swords) both being the traditional weapons of Wing Chun system.

A basic breakdown of the Sil Lim Tao form.
The 1st section of the Sil Lim Tao form trains qi sao concepts, training the breath, movement of Qi and how to correctly use the elbow to drive the arms forward in the correct position toward the target area.

The 2nd section teaches Gum sao with the concept of side stepping out of the force and practical self defence.

The 3rd section is about upper and lower gate coverage, using tan/garn/bon and stepping to redirect and avoid forces.

Chapter Two

Stances, Footwork and There Positioning

The footwork in wing chun is based on science, is very simple and sticks to the principle of economy of movement. The goal in combat is to be able to take the minimum amount of steps in for attack and out for defense to enable it to be effective. The Jee Shin Wing Chun system follows this principle and uses footwork to its advantage.

The system has a neutral stance, left and right side neutral stance, left and right front stance, footwork is made up of half steps, full steps, (forward and back), the side step and exchange step.

In all stances and footwork the body will be turned on a slight angle to eliminate the target area. The centre of gravity will be dropped by bending the knees and the feet will be kept shoulder width apart with 45 degree angles to the front.

When stepping keep the centre of gravity dropped at all times, this will keep you grounded and balanced. It will also eliminate giving your opponent information that you are moving in or out when the head bobs up and down as you go to step.

Whenever stepping, circular footwork will be used to protect the groin and enable the practitioner to interrupt his/her movement with balance while advancing, retreating or evading.

The feet are kept shoulder width apart for balance and mobility. The wider the stance the harder it is to step with speed and dynamics, therefore limiting one's mobility. In the ancient days Chinese women wore tight long dresses making big steps impossible and high kicks totally impractical and unladylike. We must always remember that this system was developed by a woman, Yim Wing Chun and has unique principles to female defense.

We will lightly cover each stance.

The Neutral Stance (photo 15) is used in training the Sil Lim Tao and is predominantly used in defense against weapons, or when one does not want to go to guard and give an arm or leg up as a target.

This stance enables the practitioner to be totally uncommitted, but very square on to the opponent making all targets available.

The **side neutral stance** (photo 16) is the preferred WC non contact starting stance, because the practitioner is not committed in any one direction and does not give the lead leg up as a target.

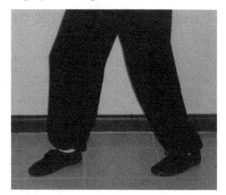

| 15) Neutral Stance | 16) Side Neutral Stance |

Both feet are parallel facing 45 degrees to the front, the body is turned in that same direction to eliminate the target, giving us a lead shoulder, this lead shoulder designates the lead side.

In this stance left and right are designated by the arms, because there is no lead leg forward to refer to as a reference.

The lead leg, under the lead guard is the preferred kicking leg, but with a small shift in balance the opposite leg can be used. This stance is used at non contact range, allowing for defense or attack, or both, without being committed to one specific side.

This stance enables the practitioner to side step (photo 21) any force that comes straight in through the centre, avoiding any force on force with the opponent.

From a side stance, circular stepping forward or back will bring you into a left or right front stance.

The front stance (photo 17) is on a 45 degrees to the front, with one leg in front of the other on a 45 degree diagonal to the front, feet are shoulder width apart, with the toes facing 45 degrees to the front, the body is turned slightly to eliminate the target.

| 17) Front Stance | 18) Equality of arms |

Keeping this stance on a diagonal helps to protect the groin and allows for the equality of both arms (photo18) through the centre line, enabling both punches to reach the target whilst staying balanced, yet still eliminating the target area slightly.

If we had an imaginary line running through the centre of both feet, the lead toe and rear toe would be roughly 5 centimeters off either side of this line, giving us our 45 degrees to the front. This diagonal maintains the idea of a triangular base.

When a non wing chun combatant lines up in a front stance with his left foot forward, he is referred to as an orthodox fighter. This means that he is right handed and he is going to jab at you with his weak lead left hand, waiting for the opportunity to use his right hand which is the power punch from the rear.

The opposite applies when a person lines up on the right side, he is referred to as a southpaw fighter. He is left handed and will jab with his weak right hand, awaiting the opportunity to king hit from the strong rear left arm.

This is the science of fighting and if a practitioner knows this about his opposition, it allows him to be one step ahead of the game.

The wing chun practitioner will attack off the lead arm regardless of whether he is right or left handed. Because he is trained to fight equally on both sides, he is able to choose whether to line up orthodox or southpaw.

Being able to change sides in combat not only confuses your opponent, but allows you to dictate the fight by eliminating some of his options. This strategy is very handy in full contact competition.

A **full step** forward (photo 19) or back from the front stance would only be initiated if the opponent took a full step forward or back, allowing you to change sides with safety. It is not a necessity to change when the opponent changes, just an option.

19) Full step forward from a left front stance to a right front stance using circular footwork

Changing from left to right is a great strategy for confusing your opponent, or when you want to remain in the parallel leg (photo 22a) or cross leg (photo 23a) position with the opponent. In other words when he changes sides you also change sides sticking as close as you can.

To apply a full step forward, (photo 19) keeping the knees bent, open the lead foot and transfer your weight onto the front foot, circle the rear leg in close to the ankle, whilst changing guard then step forward on a 45 degrees to the front, adjust the back leg to maintain balance and width. We call this circular footwork. To take a full step back one would open the rear leg, transfer the weight as the lead leg circled back into the ankle and back out on a 45 degree angle, finishing with adjusting the front foot.

Circular footwork is used in all stepping, except multiple half steps, this is to allow for the interruption of footwork with balance. Circling the feet also give us protection of the groin and enables us to place our feet down where we choose, giving us the best positions in relation to our opponent and helping us to control our own destiny in combat.

Circling the feet gives the practitioner great speed for the interruption of movement in combat. Allowing the practitioner to interrupt his/her movement and place the feet down at any instant while maintaining their balance, giving them total control over correct distance and positioning.

Half steps are small steps used to go from contact to exchange range, when we need to chase and stick to our opponent or for small retreats away from the opponent when in trouble.

In Wing Chun when the force comes in, one must retreat enough to allow for the correct range, non contact, so as the punch or kick etc will not be able to hit you.

A small half step could be utilized in this situation and in accordance with economy of movement, the rear leg would half step away giving you the correct safe range from your opponent, while the lead leg would circle back into the ankle and then forward taking you back into the correct distance and position for attack. This would eliminate the need to take a half step back with both feet for retreat and then a half step forward with both feet to attack, instead of taking four steps, you would only need to take two steps, one back and one in, saving valuable time.

Half steps give the wing chun system great dynamics with footwork, allowing the practitioner to move and shift with great bursts of speed in any one direction.

Exchange step (photo 20) allows the practitioner to change from a left or right front stance to the opposite side (southpaw or orthodox) without crossing over the centre line and exposing vulnerable targets. It also enables the exponent to yield to forces whilst coming back into a position of advantage.

20) Exchange step from a left front stance to a right front stance

From a front stance the front leg is placed behind the rear leg into a T position, (photo 20) which is referred to as a T stance. The weight is placed on the rear foot allowing the individual to kick off the front leg from the T stance, or step forward on the opposite side to attack.

The side step (photo 21) is initiated from a side stance. Either leg is placed behind the other to create a T stance. The side step enables the practitioner to avoid the oncoming force and change direction extremely fast. From this position the practitioner can kick or step up into exchange range.

21) Side stepping to the left

Ensuring that the rear leg steps across and not forward, the side step can also be initiated from a front stance with the rear leg stepping across and the lead leg adjusting back to create the T.

If one should move the rear leg forward from a front stance, up to the lead leg to create the T, then the practitioner has moved forward into the attack, changing the range and creating a force on force scenario.

Range and distance will be covered in the five stages of combat.

All steps will land on the ball of the foot first, then the whole foot will be placed down, when it is safe to do so. Landing on the ball of the foot enables the practitioner to pick the foot up as soon as it touches the ground, allowing for a quick interruption of one's movement if necessary.

When a practitioner lands on the heel first, he is completely committed in having to place the whole foot down on the ground before he is able to pick the foot up again. Making him far too slow and heavy footed, with no economy of movement.

Plus landing on the heel encourages the foot to face the front exposing the groin instead of being 45 degrees to the front which protects the groin.

This simple but decisive footwork must be mastered for dynamics and safe positioning in combat.

Positioning.

The Jee Shin system is critical on the position one should take at a non contact position when lining up to, and moving in on an opponent.

When the parallel leg position is taken (both lead legs on the same side photo 22a) the wing chun practitioner will make sure that his lead leg is lined up on the outside of his opponents lead leg or foot. Moving in from non contact to contact stage the practitioner would take a diagonal path to get around the opponents lead leg and arm finishing the forward movement around the heel area (photo 22b). Keeping a buffer space between you and the opponents body. Moving any further behind only brings you closer to the opponents spinning attacks.

When the cross leg position is taken (both lead legs are on opposite sides photo-23a) the WC practitioner will line up just inside the lead toe, again taking a diagonal path in on the opponent to contact range, at the wrist and then to exchange range at the elbow, just inside the lead toe (photo 23b).

Again keeping a buffer space between the two bodies.

22a) Parallel leg   22b) exchange range position

23a) Cross leg position   23b) Cross leg exchange range position

The wing chun practitioner makes use of moving in and out on diagonals. Moving in on your opponent, or bridging the gap on diagonals allows you not to meet the force head on when coming into contact range and exchange range.

Stepping away on diagonals also takes you out of the line of force.

The WC practitioner can also step straight in to contact range and not use a diagonal when wanting to blitz the opponent with speed, whilst still maintaining the superior positions that we have talked about, inside and outside the lead toe.

Using the **Parallel leg or blind side** (photo 22a/b) of the opponents body, gives the WC practitioner the advantage of only having to deal with one arm at one time, whilst taking the **Cross leg** position means the WC practitioner is in the centre and will have to deal with both arms at the one time. They both have their advantages in combat and understanding the theory behind them both, will give you the knowledge to choose the most advantageous position for any situation.

Focusing on the elbows and the centre of gravity.

The Wing Chun system is based on bio mechanics, (the science of the human body) meaning the natural movement of the human being. All movement is initiated firstly from the centre of gravity, the core, therefore the JSWC practitioner will focus at the centre of the body on the elbows which anatomically lie at the centre of gravity (photo 24).

24) Focus on centre—elbows

When an opponent has an intention to attack, it will be magnified through his body movement, especially his elbows. The elbows will always move first to signal an intention. Plus all weapons, hands and legs emanate from the centre of gravity.

The elbows move four times slower than the fist when initiating a round punch and 2.5 times slower when executing a straight punch. Therefore it would seem logical to focus on the slower objects, being the elbows, as opposed to the faster moving fists. The hands move quicker than the eyes, this is why we have such great magicians in the world.

The wing chun guard facilitates this by never blocking the vision of the opponents mid section of the torso, we are then able to stay focused on the elbows at the centre of gravity underneath the guard, whilst still protecting the head.

The wing chun exponent has the option to change this guard, remember the basic guard is only to defend, as long as he maintains the ability to see the opponents elbows the guard becomes flexible. When a practitioner decides to change his guard, he must be fully aware of the openings he creates for his opponent when he does this. Wing chun people use this as a strategy, to lure the opponent into what they think is an opening in our defenses.

The science of the human body is such; knees will always be underneath the elbows, feet below the knees and groin above the knees. The floating rib area is behind the elbow and the ear and nose above the elbow. The wing chun practitioner knows all this and more through focusing on the elbows and the centre of gravity. Through focusing in this area the wing chun exponent is able to attack from the feet to the head without shifting his gaze once.

Wing Chun empty hand weapons.

The wing chun system uses the entire body as a weapon.

We will start with the basic weapons and move on to the more advanced.

Due to the wing chun system utilizing centre line theory, the **straight punch** takes the straight line path and is the predominate weapon. The wing chun straight punch, is a vertical fist driven by the elbow, with the whole body behind it. The fist is a complete extension of the arm while aiming the bottom three knuckles to the target area (photo 25).

25a) Wing Chun Fist   25b) Wing Chun Fist

It is very important to make sure that the elbows stay down and the wrist is not kinked in any way, otherwise serious damage to the wrist can be incurred. Exploding from the centre with the whole body behind it and using the complete arm as one extension is what gives this punch its strength.

The target on the front of the face is the nose and the ear on the side of the head. It takes 2lbs of pressure to drop someone when hitting them in the nose and 4lbs of pressure to drop someone through hitting them on the ear.

The heart, sternum, lower abdomen are also excellent targets for multiple straight punches.

When this punch is used in multiples (photo 26) it is called **chain punching,** and occupies the centre line. With the correct stance the body can still be turned slightly to the side eliminating the bodies target area.

26) Wing Chun Chain Punches

The practitioner must be careful not to roll the punches into a circular motion, they must remain linear thrusting straight forward for maximum power and effect.

Rolling the punches in a circular motion is a common error with wing chun practitioners.

Multiple straight punches have a devastating effect on the brain when the front of the face (nose) is hit. Through the speed of the straight punches, the brain is literally slammed against the back of the skull, twice in concession, causing instant knock out.

Multiple punches to the heart centre or sternum area can be detrimental to the point of causing a heart attack, after all these are dim mak points. Attacking the sternum area also attacks the core structure of the body.

Using multiple chain punches is synonymous with using a battering ram on a wall or door, there is only so much the door or wall can take before it collapses.

The Jee Shin system trains upper gate punching and two level punching, (upper gate and lower gate targets) using two arms for multiple punches or one arm for single multiple punches into the upper and lower gates.

The single arm punch takes the centre line, using central line theory and allows the body to turn completely side on, eliminating the target even more, making the single arm punch a longer weapon than the multiple punches, allowing for more reach whenever it is required. When the single arm punch is used the rear guard will be raised on the outer gate of the central line path to protect the head area. (photo-7)

The Jee Shin system also uses the **back fist** (photo 27), **Phoenix knuckle** (photo 28), **Panther strike** (photo 29) and **Tiger Claw** (photo 30) for pressure point attacking; Dim Mak.

Elbows and **knees** are utilized at the closer range. Wing Chun's devastating elbows take a circular path and are introduced in the last traditional from, referred to as the deadly form of Biu Gee, along with the lethal art of **thrusting fingers**.

The deadly art of Biu Gee, is the last traditional form in the wing chun system.

Thrusting finger strikes (photo 31) are used on soft Dim Mak targets around the body, for example the neck, groin, under the arms, into the floating rib area, all containing pressure points for the disruption of internal energy .

27) Back Fist

28) Phoenix Knuckle

29) Panther Strike (Tarn Sao)

30) Tiger Claw

31) Vertical Biu Gee Strike

31) Horizontal Bui Gee Strike

The eyes can also be used as a target, but one must remember that they are a very small target, surrounded by the strongest bone in the body, the skull, giving the practitioner a good chance if he misses, of breaking his own fingers in the process.

Thrusting the fingers into someone's eyes is an extreme act of aggression which is liable to blind them; taking someone's sight is something that you will have to live with for the rest of your life.

The deadly art of thrusting fingers should only be used in life threatening situations, they are emergency techniques and should never be used lightly or haphazardly. This part of the art is only taught to dedicated, conscientious students who reach the Biu Gee level.

N.B. One should have Dim Mak antidote knowledge to enable the practitioner to revive or aid the victim of a Biu Gee strike in recovery until an ambulance arrives. This is your ethical responsibility if you choose to use Dim Mak on your assailant.

The head butt is also used as a weapon to strike the nose when range permits.

Kicks

Utilizing economy of movement with the straight line, the **front kick** is Wing Chun's main kick and will predominantly be initiated from the front leg as it is the closest weapon. (photo 32) The ball of the foot, the heel of the foot, the whole foot, and the point of the toe (with shoes on) into the lower shin area, are all used in front kick attacking.

Wing Chun also uses the **side kick**, (photo 33) the **stomp kick** (photo 34) on the lower legs, for breaking or collapsing the knees, **jams** (photo 35) to intercept kicks and steps, and **sweeps** to the calf, feet and ankles for take downs.

32) Front Kick

33) Side Kick

34) Stomp kick

35) Jam

36) Low Round House Kick

The Jee Shin system will also utilize **low round house kicks** (photo 36) to the legs and knees when the opportunity arises, especially attacking the Gall Bladder meridian.

High round house kicks are not used for they lack any economy of movement, Wing Chun kicks rarely go above waist height.

The **heel** of the foot will even be used for stomping on the opponents instep or toes, hitting tender pressure points, stomping on the top of the knee and even using the blade of the foot to scrape down the shin bones.

A basic breakdown of the Sil Lim Tao form.

The 1st section of the Sil Lim Tao form trains qi sao concepts, training the breath, movement of Qi and how to correctly use the elbow to drive the arms forward in the correct position toward the target area.

The 2nd section teaches Gum sao with the concept of side stepping out of the force and practical self defense.

The 3rd section is about upper and lower gate coverage, using tan/garn/bon and stepping to redirect and avoid forces.

Chapter Three

The Five stages of combat

Combat is comprised of different stages, with specific things happening at each of the different stages or ranges of the combat interaction. Having the knowledge of what can happen at the different stages/ranges of combat allows one to go from A (non-contact) to C (exchange range) with much more confidence. Wing Chun has a great understanding of the stages in combat and has categorized them into five with theory on the science of each stage. Understanding these ranges or stages of the fight is imperative to being a successful Wing Chun practitioner.

These five stages of combat are;

1. Non contact

2. Contact

3. Exchange range

4. Pursuit

5. Retreat

Non Contact Stage is the first stage of combat, being that you still have quite a bit of distance between you and your opponent, you are both unable to touch one another with kicks or punches and no-one has committed to an attack.

It does not really matter what stance you are in if you cannot touch one another, but it does give your opponent information about your fighting method. The neutral stance or side neutral stance would be the optimal stance whilst at the non-contact range as it is a non committed stance.

37a) Neutral stance hands out to sides
Correct hand position

37 b) Neutral stance hands in front become a target.
Incorrect hand position

The Neutral stance is the ideal stance for dealing with an opponent with a weapon, because it is a balanced stance and it gives mobility in either direction. The hands would be held out to the sides, (photo 37a) keeping them back, level with the body and out of the way of becoming a target. Holding the hands out in front of the body, will enable your opponent stay out of range and use the hands and arms as the target area, instead of the body and head. (photo 37b). Keeping the correct stance, with the arms and hands held back level with the body will ensure that the attacker must come into range and commit to the attack with the weapon. Having the opponent come into range will allow you to be able to deal with the attack.

Having the palms facing up is a universal phoenix, signaling that I am a passive person and do not want trouble, all creatures use this non aggressive posturing when they do not want to fight, e.g. canines will lay on their backs paws up when hassled by an alpha male or female.

The side neutral stance (photo 16) is the preferred stance when dealing with empty hands, (no weapons) it is a non committed stance and enables you to turn sideways to eliminate the target area from your opponent.

This stance does slightly favour one side but with a small transfer of weight or a small swivel of the foot, you are able to use either of your longest weapons (your legs) for your first line of defense in combat if your opponent comes into your attacking range.

This stance also gives you the opportunity to side step (photo 21) out of the line of force, in either direction as the opponent comes into your space to attack.

38a) Biu sao entry

38b) Fut sao entry

38c) Bon sao entry

For you to attack your opponent from this non-contact stage, you would need to bridge the gap or space between you and your opponent with a step, a kick or a specific entry technique (photo 38a/b/c are some examples) to seek the bridge to the opponent, the bridge being the point of contact with your opponent's arm.

Contact Stage is designated by the wrist (photo 39a), your wrist level with your opponent's wrist (if the opponents arm was out stretched). The opponent is unable to reach the body or head with a kick off the front leg, without stepping at this distance (photo 39b); he can however just flick the lead leg. The combatants are also not able to strike any major targets on the body or head at this range, if attacking off the lead arm, without stepping.

It does not matter how tall or short either person is: this theory is the same for all sizes, for this is the science of the human body.

39a) Contact stage – wrist at wrist 39b) Contact stage – showing no contact with the kick

This makes it a safe range to be at when in combat, if you understand and can apply this range correctly.

This is the perfect range to be in if someone has attacked you and you don't want to hurt them, but you need to defend yourself, it might be a friend, a family member, a drunk or someone who is just being a pest.

The opponent can however reach with the rear leg and rear arm, but must lean and make a gross movement to enable them to do this. Through focusing on the elbows or centre of gravity and with Qi Sao knowledge these gross movements are very easily detected.

Once contact has been made and a bridge created, Qi Sao knowledge will be applied. It is at this stage that the WC practitioner will try and control the opponent's wrist and manipulate their balance.

This range is firstly trained with the opponents arms held out, so as one can begin to understand the distance, then it is further trained when bridging the gap on the Muk Yan Jong (Wooden Dummy). This is just one of the concepts in the first movement in the 108 Wooden Dummy sequences (photo 40).

40) Finding correct distance Correct distance – out of kicking range

In a real altercation the opponent may not have an outstretched guard, this means you need to know this range when there is no arm to gauge the distance from. Repetition in training the correct range on a person and on the Wooden Dummy will instill this distance from the body, into the eyes and brain, enabling one to reach the right distance with no arms to gauge it from, whether the opponent is stationary or moving.

From the wrist, the WC practitioner will move forward and seek out the elbow, which is the next stage of combat, exchange range.

Exchange range is designated by your centre line being at the opponents elbow range.

At this range both fighters are able to exchange blows with each other. It is at this range that the WC practitioner will attempt to use a simultaneous attack (photo 10), multiple attacks with straight punches through the centreline (photo 42 and 42b), try to control the elbow or trap the opponent's arms (photos 41a/b).

On the parallel leg side at exchange range (photo 42a) you only have to deal with one arm at one time making it a much safer position than cross leg. There is no need to move in past the heel of the opponent's lead leg. This will allow you to keep correct distance from your opponent without having to worry about spinning attacks coming from the rear arm or leg of the opponent.

41a) Trap arms and punch

41b) controlling elbow and palm strike

42) Parallel leg exchange range

42b) Cross leg exchange range

When going into the centre of the opponent, referred to as cross leg, (photo 42b) the target will give you the correct distance for striking. Being in the center you must now be aware that you will have to deal with two arms at one time. Your centerline would still be at his elbow range, but would be facing the target area if using multiple attacks.

Exchange range is a very explosive place to be, for you and the opponent, it is the range where blows can be exchanged by both people.

Do not touch knees at this range and make sure of correct position to protect the groin. Note the correct position in photo 43a and wrong position in photo 43b/c.

43a) Exchange range correct position – groin is protected.

43b) Exchange range incorrect position the groin is open

43c) Opponent kicks the groin

It is in the centre that the WC practitioner will unleash an explosion of straight punches to the centerline targets attacking the core structure of the opponent; it is also where a multitude of Dim Mak points (pressure points) become available to the WC practitioner.

When one opponent is very tall and the other short, the smaller or shorter person's advantage for attack is in the center, where there are openings, as opposed to the parallel leg side. Staying on the parallel leg side to attack, the shorter person must deal with and try to get past the opponent's longer lead arm and especially the longer lead leg, making the parallel leg side much harder to find an opening to attack through.

While if defending, by staying on the parallel side the practitioner stays away from the rear arm and therefore only has to defend against one arm at the one time. It also keeps him away from the rear leg attack.

This is one of the reasons why it is so important to know and understand the strategies of both parallel leg and cross leg combat, for the outcome of the actual combat to be successful. Practitioners cannot afford to place too much emphasis on the parallel leg side and ignore the cross leg position, and vice versa, as both are very important in actual defense and attack. When one only majors in one side for fighting, it creates a total imbalance and a major weakness in the fighting system.

The smartest empty hand fighting system in the world, Wing Chun, should not be infiltrated with such basic flaws.

The last two ranges, pursuit and retreat are trained in the last form, Biu Gee.

Pursuit is applied when the force retracts/retreats; once contact is made our arm sticks and follows the retreating energy of the opponents attack back to the target area to strike.

Pursuit also applies when the opponent tries to retreat when in trouble. Retreating will give him/her the chance to regain some space back from the opponent. The WC practitioner will try and stick with the opponent using half stepping. Sticking is a Qi Sao concept. By sticking with the retreating opponent or force the WC practitioner will put pressure on the opponent, continuing to smother their space, not allowing any time or distance to be made between the two fighters, therefore making retreat impossible for the opponent.

If a gap is made between the two combatants the WC practitioner will use an explosive kick or entry technique to blitz the opponent, bridging the gap and shutting down any space that has been created. The WC practitioner will continually put pressure on the opponent's centreline whilst trying to get back to exchange range. This strategy, takes away the opponents space that they have tried to create from their opponent and gives them no time for offense. The Wing Chun practitioners relentless forward intention is exasperating for the opponent as they try to retreat.

It is very easy to upset your opponent's balance by attacking the centerline, the core structure when they are trying to retreat. Wing Chun concept – when the force retreats, attack.

Another option when the person retreats is to launch the body at the opponent's centreline with an explosive entry technique, disrupting the opponents balance dramatically, even to the point of knocking them off their feet.

Retreat happens when the WC practitioner is overpowered by the attacker and needs to create time and space between himself and the aggressor, allowing him to regroup. The WC practitioner will try and retreat out of harm's way whilst putting themselves back in a position of advantage for combat.

A variety of retreats are available to the WC practitioner, full stepping back, a retreating entry, an exchange step, or half stepping first before using one of the above steps.

By using an exchange step (photo 44b) the WC practitioner is able to retreat out of the line of force from the attack into an attacking position (photo 44a/b/c). This can be done from either a parallel or cross leg position (photo 45).

The Wing Chun practitioner is able to use a long range retreat or a short range retreat depending on the situation.

These are the five stages of combat in Wing Chun, your knowledge and understanding of these different ranges of combat and what can happen at these different stages of fighting will mean your success or failure in combat with the WC system.

44)Hook punch coming in parallel leg

44b) Retreat from punch with exchange step to the centre

p-44c) then front kick through the center

Your mastery of position and your understanding of this science of fighting in WC at these stages can only be mastered by repetition, repetition, repetition.

45) Hook punch coming in parallel leg side—retreat from punch with exchange step to the centre

Step in and punch

Forward Intention

This is one of the most important concepts to develop in the Wing Chun system for close range combat. Training forward intention begins immediately with the Sil Lim Tao form. Forward intention must be developed in Tan, Fuk, Wu, Biu, Garn and Bon Sao, for the success of these important hand techniques to be employed.

Tan Sao (palm up block) has forward intention to redirect any strikes or force coming in through the centre. Tan also has forward intention in Qi Sao, straight to the chest if there is no force to stop it (photo 46).

Fuk Sao (bridge on arm) trains forward intention for use in Qi Sao, Fuk must redirect and control the energy, or attack coming in toward the chest under the Fuk Sao from the opponents Tan Sao (photo 47).

Wu Sao (guarding arm) trains forward intention, not in a rigid way but alive, like a spring ready to explode forward if an opening is found (photo 48).

Biu Sao (thrusting arm) has forward intention as it is thrust out across the upper gate to find and redirect attacks coming in through the central line, it is also used as a feign or distraction (photo 49).

Karn Sao (pronounced Garn, splitting block) has forward intention to redirect forces off the centre coming into the lower gate (photo 50).

Bon Sao has forward intention in that it does not collapse, but yields when redirecting forces coming in through the centre above the arm (photo 51).

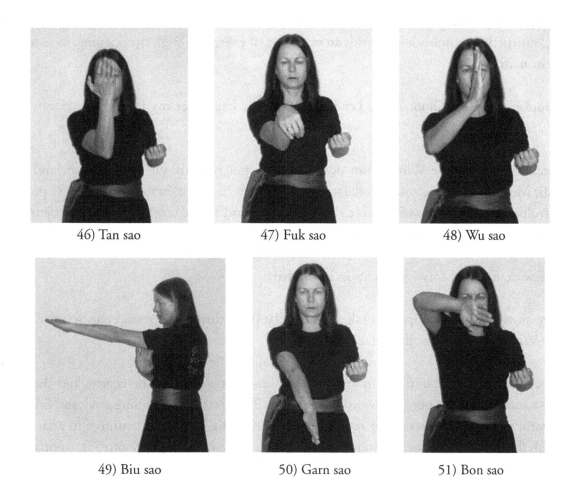

46) Tan sao   47) Fuk sao   48) Wu sao

49) Biu sao   50) Garn sao   51) Bon sao

The elbow is the driving force behind all these movements and the energy must be kept very springy, not tense or rigid. These movements must be alive, to enable them to pick up the information being transmitted through the contact point or bridge. This allows you to make a split second decision whether to redirect the attack, yield or explode forward.

Intention is the catalyst behind everything we do in our lives; nothing living takes a movement without there is intention first.

Having forward intention enable's the WC practitioner to continue to move forward overpowering the opponent by smothering, redirecting and controlling the central space between the two combatants. By having forward intention, while covering the centre, the WC practitioner will eventually find a hole in the opponent's defences and find the path with the least resistance to the target area; or the practitioner will find contact with the opponent through their forward intention, enabling them to control the arm and create their own opening to the target area.

This forward intention can be likened to water; water flows forward on its path until confronted with an obstruction, it will flow around the obstruction, or over the obstruction, even through the obstruction if it has the power to do so. When its path is completely blocked it will build up pressure and seek out the weakest point, the path with the least resistance. Once the weakest point or slightest gap has been found, it will slowly begin to leak through until eventually pushing through and ultimately cracking open the weak point in the obstruction to unleash itself with an explosion of energy through the opening, so as to continue forward on its natural path.

The same applies to Wing Chun. Bruce Lee always said, 'be like water my friend'. Water can be soft or hard.

Forward intention teaches the Wing Chun practitioner to put pressure on the opponent and not chase empty hands. Meaning that once one's understanding of forces has been established, the WC practitioner's goal of controlling the centreline will enable them to go forward to the target area and not be tricked into chasing the opponent's punches and attacks when unnecessary.

These are a few examples of forward intention in combat.

When we are cross leg and the opponent takes the circular path, throwing a round punch, the centre is left open for the Wing Chun straight line attack (photo 52).

If the wing chun practitioner initiates an attack to the head, cross leg, (in the centre) and the opponent blocks the fist and deflects the punch, instead of the wing chun practitioner pulling away and finding a new target, the wing chun practitioner could retract, come around the block and continue to attack the same target through the centre or roll the elbow over and continue to attack forward (photo 53). Another option is to come under his block (Tsuen sao), control (lop sao) his arm and continue to punch forward (photo 54).

If we initiate an attack to the head cross leg but on the outside of the opponents lead arm, when he blocks we are able to go with the force, roll to control the elbow from underneath and continue our attack into the ribs (photo 55a/b)

If the opponent tries to retreat, the WC practitioner's forward intention with half stepping would enable them to stick,

52) He round punches, the wing chun person takes the straight line attack
he blocks

some of her options for defence once he blocks are

p 53) Roll the elbow forward

p 54a) come under his block, Lop sao/grab his arm and continue to punch forward

55a   55b

p54b/c) The WC person punches to the head in the centre, but on the outside of the lead arm. He blocks, so the WC practitioner goes with the force, controls the elbow and attacks the ribs.

Having forward intention does not mean going forward blindly or barging forward like a bull, it means covering the centre and dealing with whatever happens with sensitivity and feeling, enabling you to find or create a path with the least resistance, a hole in his defence, to the target area. While going forward the wing chun practitioner must be able to interrupt the movement with balance and adapt to what they are feeling and seeing during the interaction.

Major principle of Wing Chun is interrupt ability.

In nature trees that have a good foundation and bend in the wind survive the storm, those that have a week root system, are rigid and stiff usually break or have their roots torn from beneath them. The wing chun exponent trains to be firm, yet supple and flexible with a strong root to the ground.

Chapter Four

Qi Sao

Qi Sao is the heart and soul of Wing Chun; to be one with Wing Chun one must understand and master this heart and soul that is the core of the wing chun system.

Wing Chun is the study of the science of energy, and this study is developed through Qi Sao practice. We need to understand this science of energy to be able to employ Qi Sao with great efficiency in the WC system. The understanding of Qi Sao takes the WC practitioner to a completely higher level of combat. Qi Sao raises the WC practitioner to such a high skill level, he/she is able to control their opponent blind folded, simply through feeling. This is a very high level of skill to achieve when a practitioner can fight an opponent without being able to see them.

Qi Sao in WC is referred to as Sticky Hands and as this translation infers one must have contact with the opponent or partner to be able to stick to the arms enabling them to feel the force, find an opening in the opponents defence, or to trap and control the opponent's elbows and arms.

This is why contact stage in WC is such an important range. Sticking to arms and having forward intention will shut down that arm as a weapon, take away its space, making it unable to function in a free way, confusing and compounding the opponents thinking in combat.

The force or energy from a punch can only travel in one direction at any given time. Once contact is made the force will only do one of four things,

*the force will stay there, whereby the WC practitioner will remove it to create an opening to attack through,

*the force will take you off centre, whereby the WC practitioner will come back and attack through the centre,

*the force will retract or retreat, whereby the WC practitioner will pursue the retreating force forward and attack,

*the force will push in, whereby the WC practitioner will yield to the force.

Having your body understand this knowledge, raises the WC practitioners contact reflexes to exceptional speeds. Having forces programmed into your muscles, enables you to use conditional reflexes and eliminates having to rely on so many messages coming and going from the brain.

In order to learn effective self-defence skills, it is important to have an understanding of motor-skills. Essentially this helps us understand how the body responds to a given stimulus. This in turn helps us understand what techniques will most likely be effective under the stress of a real assault and which ones won't. One aspect of motor-skill research is the understanding of reflexes and instinctive responses to an attack.

Motor skill researchers break down the common reflexes into 4 basic categories and these are

M1 Reflex

M2 Reflex

Triggered Reaction

M3 Reflex

M1 Reflex is a monosynaptic stretch reflex which is the fastest of the reflexes and has only one synapse to the spinal cord. The patella or knee jerk reflex is an M1 reflex. This reflex occurs when a muscle is surprised and placed under a sudden and unexpected load. M2 Reflex is a polysynaptic functional stretch flex and has more than two synapses in the spinal cord, making it a bit slower than the M1 Reflex but still extremely fast.

The triggered reaction is slower than the M1 and M2 reflex as they contain many more synapses therefore taking longer to reach the brain. Triggered reactions are used to protect us from pain, an example is when someone touches a hot stove, we withdraw rapidly for protection. Both hands come together, one protects the other. This is the withdrawal response. Some sounds and visuals can also set off this reflex, for example when someone hears a car back firing and jumps, or some other loud noise. Someone sneaking up and touching you or jumping out and frightening you. You get startled and react.

Generally in a triggered reaction the hands will automatically move away from the source of pain or in a car accident the hands will pull in towards the centre and try to protect the head and torso from injury. These are the basic Instinctual reflexes that will take over if a person has not been trained to do something else.

These 3 reflexes above are referred to as simple reflexes and are involuntary, meaning they occur without conscious thought. They cannot be trained to improve.

The reflex we want to talk about in Wing Chun is the M3 Reflex. It is one of the slowest reflexes but is a voluntary reaction-time reflex and is referred to as a 'Conditional Reflex' by some researchers. Trained defensive or protective flinch responses fall into this category and are the reflexes that are of interest to us.

Generally the stimuli for the reaction is visual but can also be triggered by tactile or auditory cues. For example, being a passenger and seeing our car about to hit another car, tripping over, seeing another person having an accident, hearing the screeching of breaks.

In self defense it could include seeing a punch or kick coming, seeing the shoulders move or the fist being clenched prior to being launched at our head. For us in Wing Chun it is the elbow movement which will trigger our response. Fundamentally we observe the possible threat, recognize it as an actual threat and then initiate a motor-program in response.

Yet in respect to self defense or martial arts this is where things become problematic. If we have a multitude of defenses against a straight punch, another multitude for round punches, kicks, sticks and knives etc then we tend to create too many motor-programs and our reflexes will slow down while we decide which program we will use to deal with the situation. The same problem will apply if you have been training a lot of unnatural body movements. By the time a practitioner chooses the correct counter to the attack they will probably already have been hit.

The secret to correcting this problem is to endeavor to re program the M3 Reflexes into 'automatic responses' and develop them into the equivalent of Triggered Reactions'.

How do we achieve that?

We do this by training with natural gross-motor movements, minimize our defensive choices and make those choices relevant for all attacks in a variety of diverse situations. This trains the brain to perceive and identify the threat sooner. In wing chun we call it contact reflex training. Training the brain to recognize the visual and/or the feeling of the attack, therefore uplifting the ability to perceive and identify the threat sooner. Raising action reaction time. Example, instead of waiting and trying to see the punch coming at us before we react, we learn to respond to the movement the elbow creates in relation to the attack. If we have contact we react to the feeling of what direction the force is taking and the elbow visual for recognition of the attack. This can also be done with no visual, just by feeling what direction the forces are taking.

Training to listen to the verbal and observe body language should also come into play and alert us to be on the lookout for an attack. Learning to identify the verbal and non verbal cues prior to an attack allows us to respond to the cues, not the actual attack. This allows us to be 'ahead of the 8 ball', so to speak.

These basic responses are then trained repeatedly, over and over again through a variety of drills until they become a spontaneous automatic response.

If we stick to using natural movements, the skills will be based on natural neuropath ways making it easier for the average non athletic individuals to use, learn and retain.

Wing Chun is based on natural movement so this type of training is perfect for this system.

This technical information is exactly what we are discussing when we talk about training and uplifting our response time in Wing Chun. We train and condition our M3 Reflexes to respond to the forces we are going to encounter during combat, raising them to an automatic response that responds automatically on contact, more like a triggered reaction. This is what gives Wing Chun Qi Sao the edge. WC also trains the eye reflexes to respond to elbow movements.

This way the WC practitioner has a feeling and a visual reflex to work with in a dynamic combative situation.

Training starts very simply with contact to a partner, at the contact stage. Firstly we become familiar with the forces and the feelings generated from the forces we discussed above. The WC practitioner will then train to have one or two specific responses to each of those forces, which will in turn train our conditional reflexes to be automatic and more like a triggered reflex.

When we come across these forces or feelings in combat we will have an automatic response, or automatic reflex to deal with them, eliminating the entire process of having to think.

The same applies to watching the elbow movement. The elbows will make the same movements over and over again while initiating an attack or response. By embedding these movements into the mind, the wing chun practitioner is able to react on the initial movement rather than the actual attack. This puts the wing chun practitioner ahead of the eight ball so to speak.

The process of training our conditional reflexes continues with a number of drills unique to wing chun.

These Qi sao drills are;

Parallel Single Arm Qi Sao

Moving Cross Leg, Single Arm Qi Sao

And Moving Cross leg, Parallel arm Qi Sao.

Parallel Single arm Qi Sao prepares us for close range combat in the use of double arm Qi Sao.

Parallel Single arm Chi Sao Drill

Parallel Single arm chi Sao is practiced stationary from a neutral stance with a partner. It employs one moving arm and one static arm, develops contact reflexes, sensitivity, sticking to the arms and forward intention in Fuk Sao, Tan Sao, and Bon Sao.

Terminology for the Qi Sao movements are:

Fuk Sao – bridge on arm

Tan Sao – palm up block

Bon Sao – wing arm

Jut Sao – jerk hand or pinning hand

Biu Choi - thrusting punch

Jeung - palm strike

The drill trains Tan Sao, Fuk Sao, Jut Sao or Gum Sao and Bon Sao, central line theory, action reaction response, correct position of the arms, visual, sticking, independent movement of the arms and body.

The drill teaches us to use Tan Sao to create openings for attack in the upper gate, to release and stick with Fuk Sao, before redirecting the force (palm strike) coming in under the arm from Tan Sao, into the lower gate using Jut Sao or Gum Sao, also to redirect attacks coming over the arm in the upper gate using Bon Sao.

This drill develops the concepts of; sensitivity in conditioning our reflexes, strategy, close range distance for combat, the straight line attack, to attack when we control the centre, to yield and not fight force against force, to create openings and to attack using forward intention through gaps in our opponent's defenses when correct positions are lost.

This is the foundation of double arm Qi Sao and happens in a static position. Using only one arm simplifies the drill, and allows for all this information to be programmed into the arms and mind. This training uplifts our mind, body coordination while training conditional reflexes to an action, reaction response in close range combat, in the upper gate without having to think about the legs in the lower gate.

This is the first stage to Double arm Qi Sao.

Correct position of the arms is vital for attack and defense. The target area in this drill, from contact is forward using the straight line attack to the chest. On contact the arms must be in the correct position, with forward intention to keep the opponent from being able to come forward and strike the target area.

We gain the **correct position** with the both arms, by having the elbow of the **Fuk Sao** (bridge on arm) pointing straight to the ground, in front of the chest, with the inside edge of the wrist being the contact point with our opponents **Tan Sao** (palm up hand), on the centerline. This will create a straight line running from the point of contact through the elbow point to the ground (photo 55a). A common mistake when using Fuk Sao in Qi Sao is to have too much contact with the wrist and fingers; we aim for only one point of contact (photo 56b).

When the entire inside surface of the wrist and fingers are making contact with the Tan Sao arm there is too much contact (photo 56b). Too many points of contact, means there is too much information coming into the brain for it to decipher, this slows our reaction time down, thus taking away the ability for the response to the information to be super fast.

55a) Fuk sao correct position   55b) Fuk sao incorrect position

56a) Correct – one point of contact   56b) Incorrect – too many points of contact

57) Tan sao correct position   Tan incorrect – elbow in too far

The goal in single arm Qi Sao is to have one point of contact, then information is only coming in from one point instead of many, allowing us to develop our lightning fast conditional response. The fastest response we can achieve.

Fuk Sao should look the same as in the Sil Lim Tao form with fingers facing diagonally down, not sideways.

Tan Sao needs to be high enough that the forearm covers the chest, with the middle finger of the palm on the centerline. There should be a straight line from the point of contact with Fuk Sao, on the outside of the wrist, through the tip of the elbow to the floor. (photo-57) Tan should have a slightly outward slant. Again be sure not to have the elbow too far out or too far in, the elbow point should be just off center pointing to the ground. Having the elbow in too far will give your partner an opening straight to the chest.

Tan should look exactly as it does in the Sil Lim Tao form but only needs to be high enough to cover the chest.

The correct position for Bon Sao would be if we tipped the Tan Sao over pivoting on the wrist, without moving the wrist up, down or out. Ensure to keep the elbow up on Bon Sao and allow it to yield ever so slightly as it redirects in the upper gate.

The wrist should be in the centre at nose height, the elbow should be as high as your ear and the wrist should be lower than the elbow when protecting the head.

Bon Sao should look the same as in the Sil Lim Tao form (photo 59).

59) Bon sao correct position   Bon sao wrist too low   Bon sao wrist too high

Fuk Sao turns into **Jut Sao** (jerk hand) or **Gum Sao** (pinning hand) as it redirects the palm strike down into the lower gate. The Jut/Gum will redirect the arm all the way down into the lower gate, finishing in the centre, bringing the arm in slightly toward your body to take the opponents balance, lightly putting their weight on their toes as we defend.

To follow the sequence and development in single arm Qi sao see photo's 60a through to 60f. (see page 69)

It is at this stage of training that a student needs to be patience, diligent and dedicated to repetitious movements in training. Hours and hours of training need to be put into drilling these movements correctly so as the feeling of what is happening at the contact point, can be programmed into the body. In general people become bored very quickly, and once you stop paying attention, sensitivity is lost, the correct position is lost or an advantage of feeling the opening is lost when our partner's position is not correct. When focus is lost the drill becomes just aerobic movement and all the hours put into training the concepts of it are wasted. Diligence is imperative.

Single arm Qi Sao drill can and should also be practiced with no partner.

Pictures 60a to f reveal the single arm Qi sao drill sequence

60

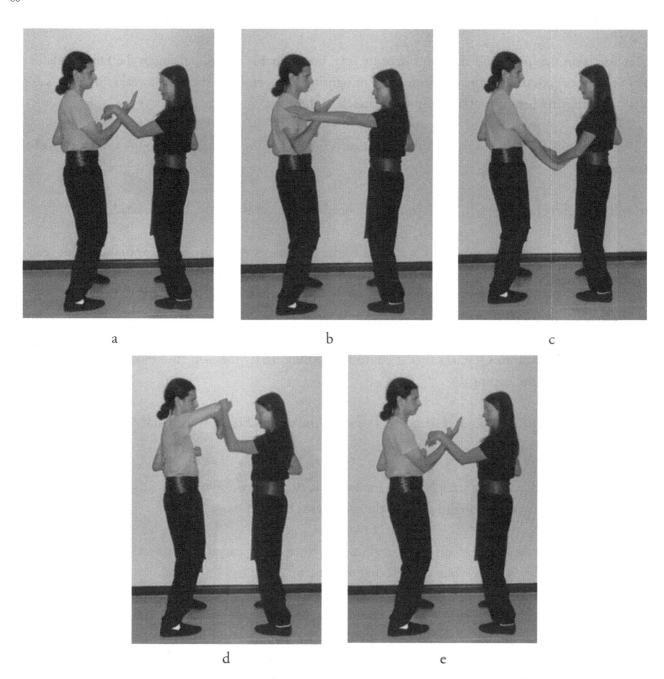

a   b   c

d   e

Below is an explanation on each of the separate movements in the drill.

a) Both wrists connect, one in Fuk sao and one in Tan sao. Both arms push forward lightly, from the elbow to make a connection and develop forward intention towards the chest. Both arms must be chest height.

b) Tan sao is on the inside and controls the centerline, but is unable to strike through the Fuk sao defence, due to the elbow controlling the centre; instead of fighting force on force the Tan sao takes the Fuk sao off centre, creating an opening with a straight line attack to the chest.

c) The concept of Tan sao in Qi sao is that it redirects forces coming straight in through the centre, off the centerline.

Tan will be slightly lower than in the form, it only needs to protect the chest, not the head.

Fuk sao releases as the opponent opens but sticks to the opponents wrist, giving no resistance. This teaches the Fuk sao to stick to the arm, go with the force and not resist the opening.

The Fuk sao could always come around the tan sao when it opens up the centre and attack the centre line.

The concept of Fuk sao in Qi sao is that it controls anything under the arm (the Fuk), or attacks coming under the arm, into the lower gate.

Tan sao turns into a palm strike and strikes in a straight line to the chest, ensuring not to deviate into an arc toward the chest.

Fuk sao feels the strike coming straight in and redirects it all the way down at the wrist into the lower gate with jut/gum sao (fingers up), slightly taking the opponents balance.

The palm strike (tan hand) feels the Fuk sao redirect the force down and allows itself to fall and go with the redirection into the lower gate, while still sticking to the arm.

Once this feeling of what the force is doing, becomes embedded in the brain and arm, you can trick your partner, by striking off the tan sao with great speed, forcing your partner to redirect it down with a lot of energy. Dictating this to happen, you are already one step ahead; you interrupt the striking movement and come over the Fuk sao redirection with your strike to the upper gate.

d) Once the jut/gum sao has redirected the palm strike down into the lower gate, it now controls the centerline as it is on top of the striking hand. The jut sao will now punch up to the head in the upper gate.

The hand that is underneath will lose contact as the punch is applied, Bon sao must rise up quickly to redirect the punch over the head, using the wrist. This is the only time through the drill that contact will be lost. If you stick at this point, it means that the hand underneath the jut/gum sao has anticipated the punch to the upper gate, rather than feeling the loss of contact as the trigger for the response. The practitioner must wait and feel the shift in contact before using Bon. This trains the feeling of the shift from contact to non contact.

The concept of Bon sao in Qi sao is that it redirects attacks coming over the arm into the upper gate.

e) The Bon sao arm, after redirecting the punch, will pivot into Tan sao, with forward intention toward the chest, along the centre line and reconnect with the Fuk sao arm.

The punching hand will turn back to Fuk sao, with forward intention along the centre line toward the chest, to reconnect with the Tan sao. Now we are back to the starting position and the drill begins again.

It is at this point that we must ensure the arms come back to their correct positions and that the energy is going forward, not up, down or sideways off the centerline. We must not become complacent, stay focused on all the points.

Qi sao is the ultimate close range sensitivity training tool; we learn what the forces are doing and how to respond to them immediately without fighting any of the forces. This drill is the beginning of your journey to reaching a very high, rare level of skill, you must be patient.

Eight Point Chi Sao Drill

The next step to double arm Qi sao is the **8 Point Drill.**

This involves combining the parallel single arm drill, both left and right sides into one drill, using both arms at the same time, while introducing footwork.

This is a very difficult drill to master; both arms are now doing two different roles at the one time. While at the same time the feet are stepping in to attack and yielding on a 45 degree angle from our partner's attack.

61) The first two photo's show the correct step back on the 45 degree angle giving the ability to use two arms simultaneously

The third photo shows stepping back with the incorrect angle which does not give the ability to use two arms simultaneously

You must step back on a forty five degree angle (photo 61) for the use of the two arms to be effective. Central line theory must be applied so you need to step and create a position where both points of contact are facing the center line, this will enable you to be in range to strike your opponent. These points being the wrist on the Fuk Sao and Bon Sao in the upper gate and the jut/gum and palm strike in the lower gate. This will give you the correct position for range to enable you to punch the target area. Importance is placed on maintaining form, balance and forward intention in both the arms and body while incorporating stepping, forward and back to attack and defend.

We are now trying to coordinate designated movement, in both the upper and lower gates simultaneously, so once again, patience is the order of the day, as it is only slowly, slowly we begin to gain control over the whole body, enabling the next level of Qi Sao to be reached. I cannot stress the amount of hours of practice required for the understanding and programming of this drill, to give us a good foundation for random double arm Qi Sao.

The eight points are designated in photo's 62—1.2.3.4.5.6.7.8.

1. One open's with tan sao, steps forward and strikes, allow the arm to drop (but stick) as your partner steps back, deflects the palm strike into the lower gate with gum sao which now controls the centre

2. Your partner steps into neutral stance, punches to the head, you redirect the punch off the centre in the upper gate with Tan Sao as you step back into a neutral stance

3. your partner will Fuk sao (both in a neutral stance)

4. Both roll changing the position of the arms

5. As your partner opens with Tan sao, Fuk Sao will release, sticking to the Tan Sao's wrist

6. Stepping forward, Tan sao will palm strike straight to the chest, Fuk sao will turn into Jut/Gum sao and deflect the strike down into the lower gate with a step back, both are in a front stance.

7. Jut sao will take advantage of controlling the centre (being on top of the opponents strike) and step forward into neutral stance and punch toward the head, your partner will step back into a neutral stance and redirect the punch with Tan Sao

8. The punch will return to Fuk sao (both in neutral stance)

1. Roll to change arms – the eight points begin again.

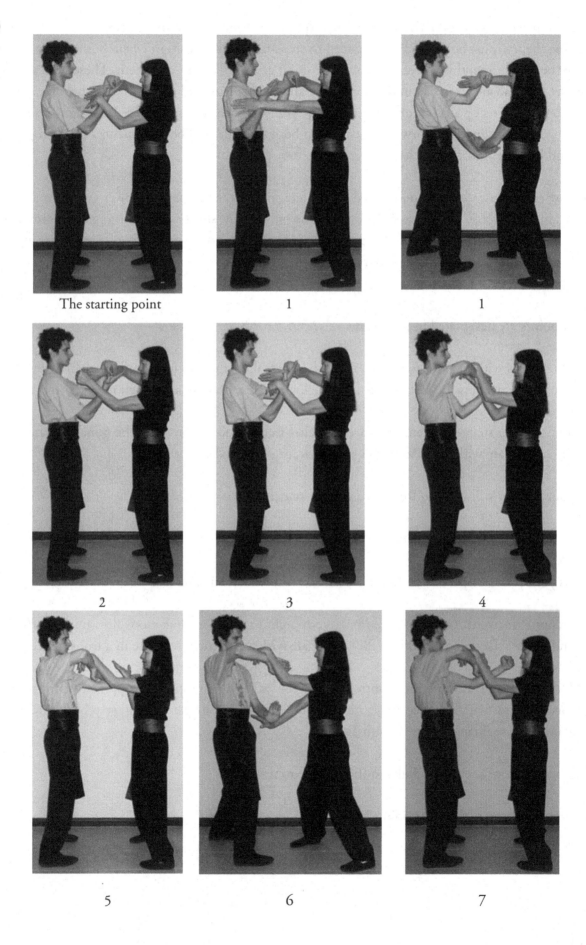

The starting point

1

1

2

3

4

5

6

7

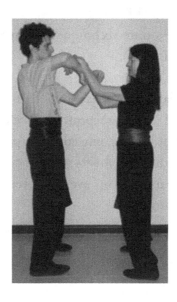

8

You will now appreciate the benefits of the many hours spent training the basic single arm Qi Sao drill.

The eight point drill humbles us, which makes us respect and appreciate the skill that we are trying to learn even more.

Common faults are:

- Elbow out or in too far on Fuk sao and Tan sao

- Losing energy in the Bon arm while working with the Fuk sao arm

- Losing forward intention as the arms roll back into the Tan and Fuk positions

- Either pushing down, sideways instead of straight forward

- Not stepping back on a diagonal. You must step back on a diagonal to allow your centerline to face the points of contact on both arms; this will enable the use of central line theory. (photo 61)

- not adjusting both feet when stepping

During the single arm drill we learn to redirect the punch in the upper gate with Bon sao, in the 8 point drill that changes and Tan sao takes over the role of redirecting the punch off the center in the upper gate.

The Jee Shin system trains three rolls during the 8 point drill, instead of one, before changing roles. Giving the practitioner extra practice training the rolling arms.

This drill can and should be practiced with no partner.

Only after many, many hours of repetition with this drill mastering coordination, range, position, two arm independence and control, do we progress onto technique in **Double Arm Qi Sao** where we will try and utilize all that we have learnt in these basic drills.

Due to the ever changing, visually stimulating, fast pace times that we live in, people find it hard to focus on one thing for too long. Slowing the mind down to repeat what we consider we already know, over and over again, takes great amounts of patience, but the ongoing continuity of the exercise, programs the movements and feelings into the body. Just knowing the movements will not help us to be any quicker, but getting your mind and body to know them, to feel the movements over and over again, will change our reflexes and make them as natural as walking, eating or playing.

Double arm Qi Sao

Double arm chi sao is the next step after the eight point drill; it is the absolute pinnacle of Wing Chun training and is considered as sparring. Rather than starting from a distance the Wing Chun practitioners will start from very close range, with contact at the wrists. The practitioners will try and attack and defend from this close contact position whilst rolling the arms.

Double arm chi sao is the same rolling arms as in the eight point drill without the pre determined attacks and defences.

When practitioners begin double arm Qi sao, specific techniques will be applied during the rolling of arms and repetitiously trained, before the WC practitioner can apply this close range fighting skill with random attack and defense confidently; from there one moves onto blind folded Qi Sao. Once this level has been reached the practitioner will have a very high level of skill and be very adept with close range combat due to the many hours spent training and conditioning the reflexes with these unique training drills.

The concept of Double arm Qi Sao is to find the path with the least resistance, to the opponent. The sole goal once touching arms in this drill is to find an opening to strike forward to the opponent and if you encounter resistance, using your knowledge of 8 point drill and the direction of forces, you will find a way forward to the target area through the use of forward intention, sensitivity, visual, redirections and even yielding if need be.

Remember that the circular path is the longest, if a person pulls away from contact to go round and attack, one must not be tricked into sticking or chasing that arm (referred to as chasing empty hands).

Always remember to go forward when your partner goes round, as the shortest path is straight forward, the straight line attack. As soon as the arm is felt leaving to go round, your intention should be to strike forward as the force retreats.

Double arm Qi Sao is like a game of chess, you have certain moves you can make as well as counter moves, but it is how cleverly you can employ those movements that will get you to checkmate.

For every action there is an equal and opposite reaction, so in the game of Qi Sao, by understanding the forces you are able to employ the use of an action, knowing in advance what the reaction will be, allowing you to dictate the play and eventually the outcome of the Qi Sao. Using this strategy literally puts you ahead of the action.

When we come across a very good Wing Chun double arm Qi Sao player, the use of strategy is now very important. Your opponent's skills will be honed like yours, making it difficult to find a path through there defences, so the use of strategy as well as all the other concepts of Qi Sao must now be employed. Without the use of strategies one will tend to rely on strength or use force against force. You cannot afford to rely on strength if you have a bigger opponent; you need to stick to the principles and concepts of double arm Qi Sao for it to be effective.

Even when your opponent is small you cannot afford to rely on your strength as your opponent can use your force against you. This is the concept of not fighting force on force.

However, when both parties have the same knowledge and can apply it with the same ability, strength will always play a factor.

Basic strategy for this exercise is taught in the single arm Qi sao drill, and then through repeating specific techniques while rolling the arms. A basic Qi Sao strategy is when the elbow gets trapped, the response would be to go to Tan sao, releasing the elbow, if the wrist is grabbed the response would be to go to Bon Sao, releasing the wrist.

Through repetition, the correct responses are drummed into the body when certain things happen or certain things are felt. Just like the motor skill researchers implied, we must drill and drill and drill the same response over and over again to learn the cues of the attack and be able to respond with lighting reflexes.

The ultimate goal in playing Qi sao is to trap your partner's arms or take them to the ground, while you still stand.

When training the practice of **specific technique** with a partner in Qi sao it is important not to fall into the trap of going that one step further with the technique. This takes you into untrained territory and is when practitioners start to fight force on force or start slapping with both hands and bad habits are created. When this happens all that was being trained is lost.

Both people need to accept that there must be a winner and a loser **when training specific technique**, each will have their turn. Both must be patient and allow each other to apply the technique to the finish off without having our partner resist and want to be the winner. Training partners must be humble, rid themselves of ego and allow their partner to train the technique and become the winner. The feelings and the responses can then be programmed into the body without any resistance; to be used later in random situations when our skills have been raised and honed to a higher level.

Double arm Qi Sao prepares us for the push and shove that happens during real close range altercations.

The above Qi Sao drills teach the WC exponent to stick when necessary, to the opponent's arms, thus the name Qi Sao, sticky arms.

Cross leg, cross arm Qi sao drill

Wing Chun also has a single arm moving fighting Qi Sao drill that helps us to deal with the punching and kicking encountered in combat.

Wing Chun is renowned for its ability to attack and defend simultaneously.

Cross arm, cross leg Qi Sao is a moving, traditional, conditional reflex drill, **teaching us to attack and defend with one arm (instead of two),** from the centre, or the cross leg position and uses the principle of going with the force.

When your opponent pushes you off centre from contact, instead of coming back and attacking through the center, as discussed in the forces, you can rotate in the same direction the force is pushing you.

By using large rotations to pull away as the force pushes you off centre, you can continue to circle around and come back up on the inside to cover the centre line in the upper gate (photo 63a).

The cross arm Qi sao drill employs large rotations trained in the Advanced Sil Lim Tao form, these large rotations give the wing chun practitioner coverage in the upper and lower gates.

Both people will train the left and right sides and alternate roles.

63a)

Force pushes you off center　　　　　go with the force

circle back up to control the center

Terminology for cross arm qi sao;
- Wu sao – guarding arm

- Huen sao – rotating hand

- Jut sao – jerk hand

- Tan sao –palm up block

- Karn sao – Sweeping or splitting block (Karn is pronounced Garn)

64) these pictures reveal the sequence for the cross arm, cross leg Qi sao drill

a   b

a) Both start in guard arm, light forward intention

b) she pushes him off centre and palm strikes the face, he goes with the force,

c

d

c) he does a large rotation to come back up to redirect the palm strike off the centre with a Jut sao, now he controls the centre.

d) He punches into the lower gate to the centre, she sweeps across the body to redirect the punch off centre with Karn sao (Karn sao pushes forward slightly to redirect),

e

f

e) he punches high, she sweeps back up the body and redirects the punch off the centre in the upper gate with Tan sao (Tan sao pushes forward slightly to redirect)

f) they both go back to Wu sao guarding arm to start the drill again.

Common errors in this drill are:

- Opening out to the side too far, the idea is to move the hand in the direction of your partner's toes. You are actually training to lop sao (grab) the hand to take the balance, but through the drill you will just use the wrist to move the arm and are not actually grabbing. We are trying to uplift and condition the reflex as soon as we feel our opponent shift. N.B. At the moment we are not trying to grab, we are training the feeling, not the grab! The grab comes later.

- After opening the guard up to strike (photo-64b), the hand continues to follow the retreating arm down into the lower gate. Remember you only have to move the arm off centre to create an opening to strike; you have no advantage by following the arm down into the lower gate.

- Instead of sweeping (an arc or half circle) Tan and Karn in toward the body using an arc or half circle and then forward, practitioners tend to chop into the punches, which means the energy is going sideways, not sweeping forward. Both these movements have forward intention so must curve in to get the forward motion at the end of the movement for redirection of the punches off the centreline.

- After punching high instead of going back to Wu Sao the person opens from the punch position.

- Over stepping – this is a contact stage Qi sao drill – meaning you are not able to get to exchange range because your opponent half steps back, maintaining contact stage at the wrist – there is no point overcompensating with a bigger step to attack because he moves – train the concept of the drill, contact range training a normal half step. At this point in the drill we are training footwork to be light, dynamic, balanced, a quick in and out is what you are trying to achieve.

Qi Sao is all about sensitivity and the receiving of information coming in through the hands and arms, your bridge; this is where it is very important to train specific response to this information.

Qi Sao is employed whenever there is contact made, so the Wing Chun practitioner will seek out contact to feel what forces are being deployed and use their Qi sao skill to deal with it.

Cross arm Qi Sao teaches us to fight cross leg with one arm, trains central line theory, visual, wrist range (contact stage), sensitivity, large rotations, balance, footwork (half stepping forward and back), two level punching, forward intention and control of the centreline with Wu Sao, Jut sao, Tan Sao and Karn Sao, two arm mentality, independent movement of the arms, legs and body, attack and defence and developing the ability to redirect from the inside or the outside of strikes coming in through the centreline, while moving.

It is important to start and finish each movement in this moving drill; the actual starting point of the drill must be from Wu sao the Guard arm. This must be designated each time you get back to this point in the drill.

This position of the guard arms as the starting point simulates first contact with an opponent when going from non—contact range to contact range. This is the bridge to your opponent and it is from this first touch that we will feel our first force. This is why it is important to finish each of the movements in the drill; we must know where the starting point of the drill begins so we can feel what the force is doing on contact and train the reaction to it correctly. Then the correct response can be drilled into the body and uplift the relevant contact reflex of when we first make contact, or bridge with our opponent's arm.

The Wu Sao becomes like a feeler, feeling and sensing the intention of the attacking energy source. During this drill, both people are learning to attack and defend.

Cross arm Qi sao with Pak sao punch

Once the basic drill has been programmed into the mind and body, the drill advances to become harder and more complex.

The person who initiates the drill from the contact point, instead of pushing to the side to create an opening, will step in, control the elbow with a Pak sao (slap block) send a punch into the centre, either high into the upper gate above the arm or below into the lower gate under the arm (photo 65).

The individual will then repetitiously train a response to these attacks. This is referred to as **Pak sao punch;** these extras teach interruption of movement, throughout the Qi sao drill. One is learning to step into exchange range and attack, while the other learns to step away and defend the attack.

The drill will uplift your sensitivity, interrupt ability, raise your contact reflexes and hand eye coordination.

If your partner punches over the arm, you will feel the elbow being pushed down to create the opening above the elbow for the punch, and if your partner wants to punch low, you will feel the elbow being pushed up to create an opening under the arm for the attack. While you are training the feeling of the attack you will also be training your visual of the attack. It is very important for your partner to train the Pak sao up or down so you get the feeling and respond accordingly, while they learn to create the proper openings for their attacks.

You will learn how to cover both gates at the one time by using two arm defences in case your visual sense has been impaired. Eventually you will train these double arm defences blind folded to get a real sense of being blind or vision impaired.

You could have a drink, blood, sand or gravel in your eyes, it might be dark, or things are just moving way too fast for you. These are perfect examples of when to use two arms to defend in the lower and upper gates simultaneously (photo 65).

65a) He steps in and Pak punches high

b) She exchanges to outside

c) or she yields, but stays in the centre

The drill will teach the dynamics of footwork, yielding to the push and exchanging from the centre (photo 65b) to the parallel leg side (blind side) or yielding and staying in the centre (photo 65c), training the dynamics of the defence in both the cross leg and parallel leg situations.

We are able to use one arm for defence if we can see the attacks coming (photo 66a/b). Wether staying in the centre or exchanging to the blind side, the rear hand is the preferred defence, as it is free from being controlled.

66a) He attacks the elbow with Pak sao punch high

she either exchanges

or stays in the centre to defend

85

66b) He attacks the elbow with Pak sao punch low,   she either exchanges

or stays in the centre to defend

Using the theory of defence with the same arm same side, trains the other hand to be free for simultaneous attack and defence. This defence with the same arm same side applies for both the high punch and the low punch.

However, in this drill the lead arm is being controlled at the elbow, so simultaneous attack and defence is impossible, but the concept is still trained.

Once these responses have been trained and honed, Pak sao punch will be incorporated into the moving cross arm Qi sao drill and applied randomly making it a very dynamic training tool.

Individuals can train double arm defences or single arm defences, staying cross leg or exchanging to the outside.

Lop sao punch
Another variation in the cross arm Qi sao drill, is to have the attacking person grab the wrist of the lead arm, redirecting it across the body while punching high or low with the rear arm, referred to as **Lop sao punch** (photo 67).

67a) Lop sao punch high   b) defence with Pak sao Garn sao

Lop sao punch low
defence with Pak sao/ Garn sao

This drill will train a different feeling than the Pak sao punch, uplifting one's reflexes to release the arm from an attempted grab and instil interrupt ability when you cannot release from the grab. This trains the mind to defend and continue to attack rather than freezing up and struggling because one of your arms has been disabled due to the grab.

The attacking role teaches us to grab (Lop) and punch high or low through the use of the central line theory.

A variation for defence, half step back on the diagonal and use a large Huen sao (large rotation) or Fut sao (swinging arm) to release the arm from the grab. Fut sao swings down and back away from the grab, then circles back up over the head to the front so as to cover the centre line and protect the upper gate from further attacks.

If the grab is successful you have to use Pak sao in the upper gate and Karn sao in the lower gate, which is a two level block, referred to as Pak sao *Karn sao (photo 67b/c).

Pak sao punch is now able to be incorporated into the drill and applied randomly. Once familiar with this interruption, one is able to apply both Pak sao punch or Lop sao punch through the cross arm Qi sao drill. The drill has now evolved into a very dynamic training exercise.

Using ones imagination any number of scenario's can be introduced to the training drill.

*Karn sao is pronounced with a G not a K, Garn sao.

Cross leg parallel arm Qi sao

This drill is another very hard drill to master; it utilizes centreline and central line theory. It teaches both parties to attack and redirect strikes coming in through the centreline in the upper gate and the lower gate.

Small shifts and steps are used, while the body turns at the waist, using the complete body as one whole unit, a concept taught in the Chum Kieu form.

Partners start from contact, cross leg using the parallel arms, (arms are the same as parallel arm Qi sao) one person in Fuk sao and the other in Tan sao. Large Huen sao is employed to redirect strikes coming straight in from Tan sao and low Bon sao is used in the lower gate to deflect palm strikes coming into the centre from the lower gate.

This drill expands on the idea of fighting with one arm, instead of using simultaneous attacks. Teaching one person to attack and defend with the lead arm and one to attack and defend using the rear arm. Even though we are only using one arm, at certain stages through the drill, our position of facing the redirecting arm to our centre line will give us the ability to be able to use the central line and attack simultaneously while we defend.

Our bridge in this drill is the connection point between Fuk Sao and Tan Sao, the drill teaches us contact stage, range, footwork, to create openings, to stick to the striking arm and redirect it by using semi circles, the use of low Bon sao (wing arm) and using the body as a complete unit. The rear arm must be controlled at the rear guard position, continuing with the concept of training two arms at the onetime to be independent of one another while moving.

This drill is a training tool for contact reflexes, so the rear arm is not used to attack, but in real life situations we have the ability to use the free hand when applicable, to simultaneously strike the opponent with the free arm, as we redirect the striking arm.

For this reason it is very important to follow the concept of facing the blocking arm with the centre line, this is what gives the WC practitioner the ability to use two arms at the onetime to attack and defend.

Because the drill only incorporates one arm, practitioners get lazy and redirect without getting into the correct position. Meaning they do not turn the hips to face the centre line at the redirecting arm. When drilling, practitioners think they have been successful because they have redirected the striking arm, but if the correct position has been lost, the ability to use the unique concept of simultaneous attack and defence has also been lost.

Your imperative must be to turn the hips (waist) and keep the redirecting arm in the centre of the hips for the application of technique and concepts of this drill to be trained correctly (photo 68).

The drill is done without too much power and encourages a soft flexible body; hips, waste, spine, shoulders and arms with continuity in the flow of the movements throughout.

68) A step by step explanation of cross leg parallel arm Qi Sao

a

b

c

d

e

a) Partners face each other in a cross leg position; both will have the same leg in front e.g. right leg. One will use the right hand and the other the left. One will be in Fuk Sao (bridge on arm) and one will be in Tan Sao (palm up block). Touching point is the edge of the wrist and both parties will push forward ever so slightly.

b) He pulls the Tan sao back toward the shoulder to create an opening; she releases the Fuk sao hook, but sticks to the wrist. He uses the straight line attack to strike to the chest from Tan sao as he half steps in (very small shift)

c) Her wrist (fuk sao) sticks to the wrist of the palm strike; she half steps back and redirects the strike down into the lower gate with a Huen sao (semi circle) the hips will turn so the centre line of the body can follow the deflection. He sticks to the arm as his strike to the chest gets redirected down.

d) Her arm will then use the straight line attack from the deflection to strike the lower ribs.

e) As she strikes to the ribs; he half steps away and redirects the palm strike away from the body with low bon sao. Turning the hips so the centreline follows the contact point of the redirection. Don't over commit and redirect past the centre

f) He flips low Bon into Tan to cover the upper gate; she sticks with him and comes back up to Fuk sao. You will not stop at this point, but continue to flow through the movements.

Your imperative must be to turn the hips and waist and keep the redirecting arm in the centre of the hips for the application and concepts of this drill to be trained correctly.

Photo 69a/b show the incorrect positions for the cross arm chi sao drill.]

69)

a   b

a) The girl has not turned the hips to face the point of contact as she redirects the strike into the lower gate

b) The boy has not turned his hips to face the point of contact as he redirects the strike coming into the ribs

There are many other Qi sao drills in the Wing Chun system, both cross leg and parallel leg. These drills train the WC exponent to be flexible with both inside (cross leg) and outside (parallel leg) fighting while conditioning the reflexes.

Three advanced drills in the Wing Chun system are Bon sao drill, Bon sao Lop sao drill and Karn sao drill; these topics have not been covered in this book.

In this section we have covered the basic Traditional Qi sao drills in the Jee Shin Wing Chun system.

Please keep in mind that all Wing Chun systems, may not train these drills.

Breathing and Qi development

Wing Chun does not rely on strength so internal development is very important to maximise power. When there is plenty of Qi, energy, stored at the Tantien energy centre (located inside the body one and half inches below the belly button), one has enormous amounts of potential energy or Qi at their disposal, for combat and good health. This Qi is able to explode out from the centre of the body through the limbs when blocking, punching, palm and finger striking or kicking during combat.

What is Qi? Qi is translated as air, life force energy, electromagnetic energy, the stuff that binds the universe together, there are many names that can be given to the term Qi, but none of the terms can explain the depth of this word, correctly.

Qi can be obtained through many ways, but the two basic methods are pre-natal Qi given to us at the time of conception from our parents and post natal Qi obtained through breathing, eating, drinking, meditation and exercise. Mind you, it is the essence from the air, food and drink that build Qi, so fresh food and a good diet is imperative for maximum Qi development along with plenty of fresh clean air.

We are able to build and absorb Qi into our bodies from many places, the universe, planets, stars, sun, moon, earth, sky, oceans, forests, mountains, flowers, people, animals etc but especially by breathing life force air into our bodies.

Generally a reasonably healthy human body is able to go without food for up to 3 weeks and up to 3 days without water, but only minutes without life giving air.

We take this amazing function called breathing for granted; after all we don't even have to think about it, it happens on its own. People are only too happy to spend hours in the gym exercising their muscles for power and strength, so why not exercise your lungs and breathe, to maximise your power, strength and health. When the mind and body come together in meditation and breathing they become a very powerful tool at your disposal, for building Qi internally and externally for power and strength and exceedingly good health.

Power lifters are able to blow the record books out of the water, lifting enormously heavy weights and breaking PB's at competition, by using this same method of their mind, body and breath coming together as one.

One of the main concepts of the Sil Lim Tao form in the Wing Chun system is that it is a Qi developing form and this is one of the reasons it is practiced over and over again. (See chapter one for more on this subject) Correct stance, mind focus and breathing are the key to Qi development in this form.

Sil Lim Tao can be trained for up to 30 minutes, using different breathing methods; soft, light tense and hard, which will develop the Qi through the mediation on the body, breath and movement.

Unfortunately in today's modern world people do not have the patience for such slow training methods.

The Jee shin system uses two lower abdominal breathing methods in their Traditional forms to develop Nei Dan (internal energy) and Wei Dan (external energy) in the body. The two methods are referred to as Buddhist breathing and Taoist breathing.

Abdominal breathing is the key to Nei Dan Qi building. There are two common ways of breathing: Normal abdominal (Buddhist) and reverse abdominal (Taoist) breathing. Abdominal breathing is a deep breathing exercise, not like the breathing done from the chest. Correct deep breathing involves slow, deep breaths that seem to go all the way down to the Tantien. It requires that the mind be relaxed and concentrated.

In abdominal breathing the lungs are expanded and contracted by the muscles of the diaphragm and abdomen, rather than the chest muscles.

Benefits for normal abdominal breathing:

Internal Organ Massage.

In abdominal breathing the diaphragm and the muscles of the lower abdomen are constantly moving back and forth. This movement massages the internal organs, increasing the circulation of Qi and Blood in and around them. This keeps them healthy and strong, avoiding Qi stagnation, which is one of the major causes of illness.

Invigorating the abdominal muscles.

Deep abdominal breathing keeps the abdominal muscles constantly moving. Not only does this method keep the Qi circulating around the organs, but also loosens up the Qi Channels which connect the front of the body to the legs and to the back.

If you give up abdominal breathing, the Qi flow to the governing Vessel (photo 4) in your back becomes sluggish. This weakens the ability of the Governing Vessel to regulate Qi throughout the body, and allows a number of problems to arise.

Increasing the Efficiency of the Qi Flow from the Kidneys to the Lower Tantien.

One objective of Qigong practice (breathing exersises) is the strengthening of your Water Qi (original Qi), which is converted from the Essence residing in the Kidneys. The lower Tantien is the residence of this Qi. The muscular movement of the muscles in abdominal breathing, help to lead the Qi from your Kidneys to your Lower Tantien and maintain it in that energy centre. The more abdominal breathing you do, the more Qi is led, and the more efficiently the Essence is converted. Abdominal breathing acts like an engine which is able to convert fuel into energy more efficiently than normal engines can, and thereby conserve more fuel.

To Increase the Water Qi.

Once you are able to increase the efficiency of the Essence-Qi conversion process, you will be able to create more Water Qi (original Qi). Strong Water Qi is the key to successful energy practice. Water Qi is able to calm down the mind, strengthen your will, and firm your spirits. Since Water Qi is the major coolant for your fire Qi, you are able to maintain your health and lengthen your life.

This method of breathing is often referred to as Buddhist breathing. First use your Yi (mind) to control the muscles in your abdomen. When you inhale, intentionally expand your abdomen, and when you exhale let it contract. When you inhale you should gently push out Hui Yin cavity (lowest point on the torso) in front of the anus. When you exhale, hold it up. If you practice 10min three times a day, in one month you should be able to resume the abdominal breathing you did as a baby. Do not hold your breath. Breath must be smooth, natural, continuous and comfortable. Deep abdominal breathing is done from the lower Tantien, do not expand and contract the chest.

When students begin practicing the Sil Lim Tao form, they begin with this normal breath. It is important that people learn to breathe properly for everyday life. Unfortunately the majority of adult's breath from the chest, rather than the lower abdomen, which is totally incorrect, will not build Qi within the body and is quite detrimental to our physical and mental health through maintaining too much tension in the body, heart and mind.

Once basic breathing has been established, and can be coordinated with the controlled hand movements in the form, then emphasis is placed on more intention with the breath while directing the Qi through the movements with the mind during the practice of the Sil Lim Tao form.

Once the mind, body and breath can work together in the Sil Lim Tao, it is then the practitioner can start to build on filling the Tantien with energy/Qi through the practice of the Sil Lim Tao.

The second form in the Jee Shin Wing Chun system is the Advanced Sil lim Tao form.

At this stage of training one is introduced to reverse abdominal breathing for the development and direction of Qi around the body to the extremities.

This method is commonly called Taoist Breathing. Since you are moving the abdomen, you gain the same health benefits as from Normal breathing, but if practiced all the time creates too much tension in the heart and sickness can occur as a result.

However in reverse abdominal breathing, when you inhale, you draw the abdomen in and hold up your Hui Yin cavity (located at the lowest part of the torso in front of the anus) and the anus. When you exhale you gently push out your abdomen, Hui Yin cavity and anus. This is the opposite of the first method, normal breathing or Buddhist breathing.

There are many reasons for this, the major ones are:

Greater Efficiency in Leading the Qi to the Extremities

Whenever you exhale, you are expanding your guardian or external (Wei) Qi. When you inhale you are conserving your Qi, or even absorbing the surrounding Qi into the body.

Whenever we use our intention to exert power, to say push a heavy object or to blow up a balloon, the abdomen naturally withdraws.

Taoist Qi gong practitioners found that when they want to intentionally expand or condense their Qi, the abdomen moves opposite to that of natural breathing. They realized that reverse breathing could be used as a tool to lead the Qi more efficiently to different parts of the body, a bonus for martial artist, as this is what is needed in combat.

When you feel cold and wish to absorb Qi from your surroundings, you will find your inhalations are longer than your exhalations and your abdomen withdraws rather than expands.

Therefore the great advantage of reverse breathing is the ability to lead Qi to the extremities more naturally and easily than is possible with normal abdominal breathing.

Once you have mastered the coordination of mind, breath and Qi, you will be able to lead the Qi to any part of the body.

1. **For Martial Arts.**

The Taoist breath is referred to as a martial breath because it will lead the Qi more efficiently to any part of the body than any other breath. This is very important when wanting power to strike or strength to block, in that your arms and fists do not break when blocking or striking in combat.

2. **For more efficiently raising the Qi in Marrow/brain washing Qigong.**

In Marrow and brain washing Qigong, reverse abdominal breathing is the method used to raise Qi more efficiently to the brain and through the bones, than the Buddhist methods.

Be sure to keep the diaphragm dropped and the area from the solar plexus to the navel relaxed and comfortable, (otherwise you will create too much tension in this area and stagnation will occur) after a few months of practice, you will find that there is a point of compromise which allows your reverse breathing to be deep, but also allows your chest area to remain relaxed. Once you have reached this stage you have grasped the key to Taoist breathing.

In the Advanced Sil Lim Tao form students will use this method of breathing to build more Qi and learn to compress the energy in the Tantien before exploding the energy out into their strikes, using a short sharp sniff with each of the strikes.

This method builds external Qi (Wei Dan) making the body very strong while developing great power and intention when striking.

A mixture of both these breathing methods, are also used in the Chum Kieu and Biu Gee forms for the building of Qi for use in combat.

Students are encouraged to join into our Qigong classes to further their development and knowledge of Qi development.

Chapter Five

History

The true history of wing chun kung fu is still shrouded in mystery, hearsay and legend. Today, there are many theories and stories about wing chun's origins, but categorically, there is still no significant proof or evidence to verify its true grass roots.

The most popular belief is, that the idea of wing chun fighting was conceived at the Shaolin temple, and upon its destruction by the Manchu's, all the intellectual prowess fled into southern china. We do know however, by the mid 1800's, that wing chun kung fu had found its way into southern china, and established itself with the red boat opera performers of Foshan and Canton. The Red Boats Members were a revolutionary group of kung fu experts who were opposed to the Qing rule and were intent on restoring the Ming Dynasty.

It is during the time of Li Wenmao that the earliest verifiable evidence that practitioners of yong chun quan (wing chun kuen) can be found aboard the Red Junk boats:

- Wong Wah-Bo (Huang Huabao), sometimes said to have been a native of Kulo, Heshan, is generally considered the senior of the troupe. He played the Mo Sang, (Wusheng, Male Martial Lead), and was particularly skilled in the roles of General Kwan and the Monkey King, and in the use of the kwun (kwun, pole). K is always pronounced G - guan, pole.

- Leung Yee-Tai (Liang Erdi) played the Mo Deng (Wudan, 'Female' Martial Lead).

- Dai Fa Min Kam (Dahuamian Jin, Painted Face Kam), also known as San Kam (Xin Jin, New Kam), and sometimes said to have properly been Lok Kam (Luo Jin) of Jinju, Sanshui, played the Mo Ging (Wujing, Martial Painted Face), or sometimes the villainous Chow (Chou, Clown).

- Yik Kam (Yijin, Wing Gold) played the Ching Deng (Qingdan, Proper 'Female'), a virtuous leading role.

- Lai Fook-Shun (Li Fushun), also known as Siu Fook (Xiao Fu, Young Fook), played the Siu Sang (Xiaosheng, Young Male), the beardless scholar-lover.

- Cho Shun (Cao Shun), known as Dai Ngan Shun (Dayan Shun, Cross-eyed Shun), a native of Panyu, played the Siu Mo (Xiaowu, Little Martial). A former Choy Lee Fut boxer, he became a disciple of Yik Kam.

- And others, including mentions of Leung Lan-Kwai (Liang Langui), Go Lo Chung (Gaolao Zheng, Tall Chung), Fa Jee Ming (Huazi Ming, Flower Mark Ming), Fa Min Biu, (Huamian Biao, Flower Face Biu), Lo Man-Gung (Lu Wengong), etc.

Leung Yee Tai, Wong Wah Bo and Dai Fa Min Kam were 3 members of the red boats which were instrumental in establishing and structuring wing chun into forms, training sets and weapons.

The most outstanding student of Leung Yee Tai and Wong Wah Bo was the legendary Dr, Leung Jan, an herbalist, who worked in Foshan but came from Kulo village.

The most renowned disciple from Wong Wah Bo and Dai Fa Min Kam was the legendary Yuan Kai San.

Leung Yee Tai's expression of wing chun kung fu made its way to KuLo village, when Leung Jan retired back to his native home town.

Wong Wah Bo's wing chun legacy stayed in Foshan through Leung Jan's teachings, to 4 major disciples.

Dr. Leung Jan and Yuan Kai San would each forge their own brand of wing chun from Foshan to Canton and become the 2 most influential exponents in teaching and spreading wing chun kung fu in southern china, around the early 1900's.

Chan Wah Shun, known as the money changer, was a student of Leung Jan, he became renowned for creating an alternative lineage of wing chun, Yip Man, was a student of Chan Wah Shun, who is considered his only Sifu. (one Sifu, three teachers was what Yip Chun told us while visiting him in 2010). The three being; Chan Wah Shun, Ng So (head senior student of Chan Wha Shun) and Leung Bik. While Yip Man was attending university in Hong Kong, he met one of his teachers Leung Bik, Leung Jan's son and was said to have studied with him for three years. After this encounter, he too was instrumental in establishing a unique style of wing chun in the 50's and began teaching it to the general public in Hong Kong. This story is depicted in the movie "The legend is born Yip Man" where Yip Chun actually plays the part of Leung Bik.

Yip Man taught legends, Bruce Lee, William Cheung and Wong Shun Leung.

- My lineage is from William Cheung in Traditional Wing Chun, said to be the true Wing Chun fighting system taught to him by Yip Man from Leung Bik.

- Secondly from David Cheung, taught to him by Wong Shun Leung, taught to him by Yip Man. David spent 10 years with the infamous Wong Shun Leung. He then moved to Australia and trained for 18 months (1982 - 1984) with his brother William Cheung, before teaching for him from 1984 to 1989. He then left and began teaching his very dynamic version of Wing Chun. In 1991 opened his Academy in Melbourne. Like all Chinese, David loved Bruce Lee and I know this had a great impact on his own teaching.

p 70) The Shaolin Temple

A Version of History Refuted by Some.

A version of history, refuted by some, but passed down through my lineage from Leung Jan to Yip Man. Also past down by Leung Jan to his disciples in Kulo and from many other wing chun masters to their disciples, is the story of Ng Mui (mandarin) or Wu Mei (cantonese) a warrior nun, Abbess at the Henan Temple and one of the five martial elders who managed to flee the Shaolin Temple on its sacking by the Qing Dynasty in 1732 under the Yongzheg Emperor. This destruction is also supposed to have helped spread Shaolin martial arts through China by means of the five fugitive elders.

The famous five elders who fled the Shaolin Temple are

Jee Sin Sim See (which literally translates to Zen teacher) Abbot at the time of the temple's sacking. It is said that all masters of his style were called Jee Sim Sin See which could be the reason he is said to have been in so many places, over so many years after fleeing the temple.

He is said to have been a master of the wooden man, a master of strategy, the creator of Iron Cloth Qigong, the creator of Wing Chun and the founder of Hung Gar.

86 years young grandmaster Fung Chun from Kulo says that he never actually taught Wing Chun, He just helped to create it.

Ng Mui Abbess of the temple at the time of its sacking was a Dim Mak expert, Qigong expert, martial expert and said to be the founder of Ng Mui Kuen, Wing Chun Kuen, Dragon style, White crane and Five pattern Hung Kuen, inventor of the Plum Flower Posts.

Bak Mei literally translates to White Eyebrow Taoist. He was depicted in the movie Kill Bill. Said to be the founder of Golden Bell iron body Qigong and White Eyebrow Kung Fu.

Fong Do Duk was a Taoist, said to be a master of White Tiger Kung Fu, Qigong expert and a very famous swordsman with a body of steel.

Mui Hin was the founder of Five Shapes boxing and said to have had direct input into the creation of Wing Chun.

Ng Mui was said to have been the daughter of a Ming general from the imperial court, a young lady of her standing would have enjoyed the best education and the finest martial arts training available. She developed a style that was geared toward combat rather than performance, probably due to the fact that her father was a general.

Ng Mui's parents were killed in the capture of the Ming capital. She took refuge in the White Crane Temple, in Kwangsi Province, where she became involved in the anti-Qing rebellion. Leading raids on Manchu palaces, it is said she even assassinated a Manchu prince, avenging her family.

Her style was fully developed in the Ming Imperial palace before she entered the Shaolin Monastery.

At the monastery she is said to have studied Bodhidharma's Sinew Classic Change. Having this Qigong knowledge advanced her form of martial arts to 'internal status,' allowing her to elevate her personal power to a very high level, making her a very powerful martial woman.

Ng Mui was said to have been extremely proficient in martial arts from a very young age, Wudang martial arts, Yuejianquan and then Shaolin martial arts once she became the Abbess at the Shaolin temple before fleeing after it was sacked. She was also credited as being the founder of Wei Mei (Ng Mui style) Dragon Style, White Crane and Five-Pattern Hung Kuen systems.

If this were so, then all this accumulative knowledge would give her excellent and credible credentials for developing the new fighting idea (not yet named wing chun) from the temple into an explosive simple combat system. (The style she taught to Yim Wing Chun).

During the invasion of the Qing army from the north through China, the Shaolin Temple became a safe haven for fleeing patriots and people who had been uprooted from their homes and land due to the invading Qing fighting force.

The practice of martial arts had been banned by the new government, but the Shaolin monks, whom were the most formidable fighting force in the country, also wanted the return of the Ming. Therefore allowed the rebels to continue their training secretly at the temple. Many people, who had taken refuge at the temple, would have become sympathisers and joined the cause.

It is at this time that the monks realized they needed a new fighting system; one that was efficient, effective and was quick to learn. Unlike the old systems that took years to master.

Hence these masters at the temple started to create new ideas from their ancient knowledge to develop some highly evolved concepts and principles in the art of fighting based on the science of the human body instead of animal movements.

Discovering that the temple was being used by the patriots and rebels to train in martial arts and being fed up with the rebellion, the Qing government attacked the temple and sacked it, trying to annihilate the warrior monks, the rebels and sympathisers.

After the sacking of the temple by the Qing government these five masters fled south to various temples seeking refuge.

The Southern Temple was also said to have been a haven for rebels and the secret training of martial arts. A number of secret societies were formed by these rebellion forces to try and overthrow the government.

Due to the rebellion, these monks would have passed on their fighting ideas to trusted people in order to help the rebellion fighting force that was spreading throughout the country. Therefore one would imagine that a variation of the ideas from the temple would have emerged and filtered out to different disciples at different places and times creating different lineages.

Ng Mui was a warrior nun and said to have been a sympathiser for the patriots against the Qing Government especially after the destruction of the Temple. She is said to have fled to the White Crane Temple in the distant Daliang Mountains on the border between Yunnan and Sichuan where she continued to cultivate these new ideas and concepts she had been studying at the temple.

It was here that she met and befriended a beautiful young girl of fifteen, Yim Wing Chun. A rich aggressive land owner had been harassing the village and trying to force this beauty into marrying him. Yim Wing Chun's father, who owned a noodle shop knew he could not hold off the request forever without causing trouble for the village. Ng Mui suggested to her father that he set the date for six months ahead.

Ng Mui agreed to teach Yim Wing Chun how to defend herself with the new ideas she had been developing. These ideas would be quick to learn and very effective for this small girl against her large opponent. She must first promise to only pass on her knowledge to family or very trusted friends. Wing Chun agreed and began training hard; she was a fast learner and developed a very high skill in six months.

When the bullying land owner arrived back to collect her, she challenged him to combat, if she could defeat him in a fight he would leave her and the village in peace, if she lost, she would marry him and become his wife. Thinking it a joke, the land owner agreed.

Yim Wing Chun used her new knowledge of wing chun to win the challenge fight against the land owner, injuring him badly. Injured and humiliated he honoured his bet and left the village in peace.

Yim Wing Chun is said to have continued her training with Ng Mui until she died.

Yim Wing Chun eventually left the village and travelled to Guangxi where her fiancé Leung Bok Chow lived. After marrying Leung Bok Chow, Yim Wing Chun continued to refine and cultivate these new innovative ideas, into the deadly system we know today.

Yim Wing Chun also mastered the Bart Jarm Dao (Eight slash swords).

Having been developed and nurtured by women from the time it was born, the system of Wing Chun is uniquely female friendly with unique principles and no brute force required.

While on a visit to China in 2008 Master Fung Kuen from Kulo relates a story told to him, by his master Yun Kai Sam, told to him by Leung Jan, how Yim Wing Chun tried for a long time to convince her husband to learn her fighting system. He was a master in a southern style that made his body very strong. She would tell him over and over again that he did not need muscle to win in an altercation, all he needed to know was the special techniques, position and movement that was in her fighting system.

She explained how it was much more efficient than his low horse stances that created heavy stepping and relied on strong arm bridges. Her new system had a natural stance with grounding, allowing for dynamic short pursuit and retreat steps and close range body techniques with pressure point striking, leg breaking and jamming, making it much faster and dynamic than the slower Southern and Shaolin styles.

He did not believe her technique could be more powerful than his, she was far too small and of slight build.

Frustrated by his arrogance she grabbed a pile of tiles from the roof and showed him that with one blow she could break them all. He was so astonished and impressed with how his tiny little wife could generate so much power, that he began learning the style from his wife.

After her death he is said to have named the art Wing Chun in memory of her name.

Leung Bok Chau, Yim Wing Chun's husband passed on his knowledge to Leung Lan Kwai, Leung Yee Tai and Wong Wah Bo. Leung Yee Tai and Wong Wah Bo were both patriots to the Ming cause; both became famous red junk opera performers, hiding their true identities in plain sight with face paint and opera costumes as they played out their characters on stage.

Moving around the country on the junks they were able to elude the Qing soldiers and continue to help the rebellion.

Leung Yee Tai was of very slight build and played the lead female martial roles in the opera, he maintained the soft female essence and perspective of Wing Chun.

Wong Wah Bo was a very big man, said to have been the leader of the troupe who played the lead male martial roles. He was particularly skilled in the characters of The Monkey King, General Guan and in the use of the Kuan or Dragon pole.

He developed Wing Chun from a big person's perspective, using more strength and power in his technique.

Wong Wah Bo taught Leung Yee Tai the Kuan, pole and Leung Yee Tai taught Bart Jarm Dao, swords to Wong Wah Bo. These two weapons remain the traditional weapons in the Wing Chun system today.

The most outstanding student of Leung Yee Tai and Wong Wah Bo was the legendary Leung Jan who was an herbalist and lived and worked in Foshan, but came from Kulo village. He is famous for the spread of wing chun in Southern China around the early 1900's.

Learning from both these great martial artists, Leung Yee Tai and Wong Wah Bo, instilled him with both the soft and hard sides of the art. He was sought after from people around the country for his teaching methods and fighting skill. Known as the Qi Sao King he was famous for his sticky hand skill and was undefeatable in his challenge matches.

Wong Wah Bo's wing chun legacy stayed in Foshan through Leung Jan's teaching, where he developed wing chun into a more structured style by creating the 108 point system with the three forms, sil lim tao, chum kieu and biu gee, making it much easier to teach to the public.

Leung Jan eventually retired back to Kulo village where he reintroduced Leung Yee Tai's expression of the pure female version of wing chun. He refined it even more restructuring the 108 point system into the 72 point Pin Sun system, creating 12 single man training sets, Sup Yee Lo, which incorporated a number of two man training sets, called Dui Chuk.

Leung Jan also taught his son Leung Bik and the money changer, Chan Wah Shun. Both these disciples taught Yip Man, giving him an understanding in both the soft female side and the more energetic male side of the system. This enabled him to refine and perfect the system even more, eventually forging his own unique style of wing chun in Hong Kong after fleeing China around 1946, due to the Japanese occupation.

Although only a small man, Yip Man became legendary as an invincible fighter and wing chun teacher. He is renowned as the person who opened wing chun up to the public in Hong Kong and eventually the whole world.

Yip Man taught legends Bruce Lee, Wong Shun Leung and William Cheung.

Red Boat Opera members Wong Wah Bo and Leung Yee Tai had as many as 11 peers that were ancestors to other lineages of wing chun kung fu.

Wang Family wing chun lineage

Cho family wing chun lineage

Way Yan wing chun lineage

Also, outside the red boat opera, there was a monk "Dai Dong Fung" who was the ancestor of Pao Fa Lien wing chun lineage.

Please excuse me if I have not mentioned anyone, no prejudice intended.

Today Wing Chun is one of the most popular fighting systems in the world and this is due to the legacy of two warrior women Ng Mui and Yim Wing Chun.

Myths and legends are said to be just that, myths and legends, but as we are discovering through modern science and archaeology, ancient names and places of myth and legend are being found to be very true and at this point in time no one can prove this incredible story of two legendary warrior women to be untrue.

Family Tree

JEE SHIN WING CHUN
FAMILY TREE

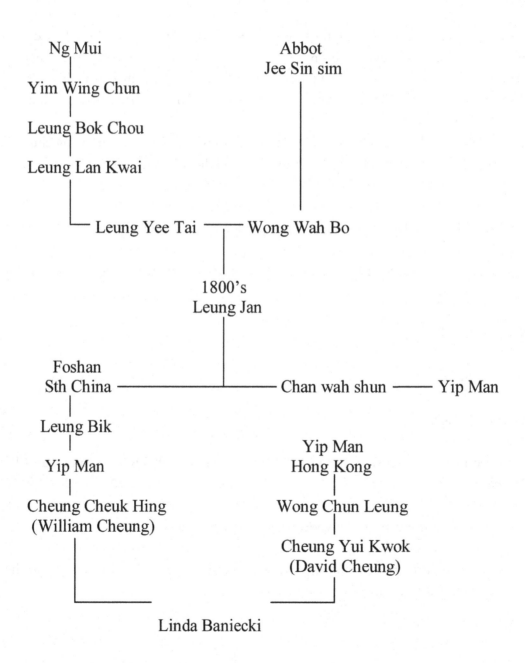

Ng Mui

Yim Wing Chun

Leung Bok Chou

Leung Lan Kwai

Abbot
Jee Sin sim

Leung Yee Tai ——— Wong Wah Bo

1800's
Leung Jan

Foshan
Sth China ——————— Chan wah shun ——— Yip Man

Leung Bik

Yip Man

Cheung Cheuk Hing
(William Cheung)

Yip Man
Hong Kong

Wong Chun Leung

Cheung Yui Kwok
(David Cheung)

Linda Baniecki

Conclusion

Wing Chun is a very practical system for the modern martial artist based on science and logic, teaching us to adapt and change with the situation. Practicing this unique system will enhance ones general health, intelligence, motor skill, focus and raise ones martial skill to one of the highest levels it can possibly reach.

Wing Chun is a thinking man's art, an art that puts brains in your muscles, not muscles in your brain.

Wing Chun is not just one of the most dynamic martial arts systems in the world, its principles and concepts are a great teacher of how people can live their lives from day to day.

WC teaches us to take the shortest path, so in life this principle should stay the same, even though most will choose the longest and hardest path in life;

WC teaches us to be spontaneous; spontaneity is the essence of life

WC teaches us not to fight force against force – teaches us to go with the flow, be relaxed and natural; even though most will go against the flow and 'bang their heads against brick walls'.

WC teaches us not to over commit, so don't give yourself impossible tasks or goals and end up beating yourself up when you cannot achieve the impossible goal you have set for yourself; be it health, fitness, finances, love, friendship, ethics or morals; keep goals simple

WC teaches us to stay balanced and focused – we should try and keep our lifestyle and psychology simple and balanced without getting overly excited or mentally run down, try and stay on a more level path;

Wing Chun teaches us to live in the moment,
so
don't dwell on the past or the future,
stay focused on the minute,
the now, today.
For it is a gift,
that is why it is called the present.

Chinese-English Glossary

Shil Lim Tao	The Way of Shaolin (little idea form)
Kuen	Fist
Bill Tchoi	Thrusting punch
Bill gee	Thrusting fingers
Sao	Hand or arm
Huen Sao	Circling Hand
Wu Sao	Guarding Hand
Lap Sao	Controlling or grabbing hand
Tan Sao	Palm up Blocked
Fuk Sao	Bridge on arm
Pak Sao	Slap block
Jeung	Palm Strike
Din Dou Jeung	Inverted Palm Strike
Po Pai Jeung	Double Hand Palm Strike
Gum Sao	Pinning Hand
Fut Sao	Swinging Arm
Jut Sao	Jerk Hand
Bill Sao	Thrusting Fingers Block
Tarn Sao	Upward Deflection Block
Bon Sao	Wing Arm

Chan Sao	Spade Hand
Chen Sao	Clearing Hand
Kan Sao	Sweeping or Splitting Block
Bon Sao	Wing Arm
Chan Sao	Spade Hand
Chen Sao	Clearing Hand
Bik Bon Sao	Elbow Strike
Man Sao	Inquisitive or seeking Hand
Chuen Sao	Slithering Arm
Lan Sao	Bar Arm
Quan Sao	Rotating Arms Block (Tan Sao and Bon Sao)
Ting Sao	Thrusting Hand (Chum Kil)
Jum Sao	Sinking Elbow block
Chum Kil	Bridge Seeking Form
Bill Gee	Thrusting Fingers Form
Muk Yan Jong	Wooden Dummy
Chi Sao	Sticky Hands
Dan Qi Sao	Single Hand Chi Sao
Sheung Chi Sao	Double Hand Chi Sao
Lok Sao	Rolling Arms in Chi Sao
Jong Sum Sin	Centre Line

Sifu	Teacher
Sigung	Teacher of Sifu
Sidai	Younger Kung Fu Brother
Sihing	Elder Kung Fu Brother
Sijie	Elder Kung Fu Sister
Sijo	Teacher of Sigung
Simo	Wife of Sifu
Sisook	Younger Kung Fu Brother of Sifu
Tong Moon	Fellow Student of Same Style

Other basic Chinese terminology

Dim Mak Pressure point

Du meridian is the Governing channel that runs up the back

Hui Yin Lowest energy point on the torso where Yin and Yang energies meet

Kuan Pronounced Guan is the Chinese Dragon pole

Nei Dan Internal energy

Pak Wei energy point on the crown of the head

Qi Breath, energy, life force

Qi gong Breathing exercises

Tantien Elixir field(energy centre)

Wei Dan External energy

Wren Meridian is the energy channel that runs up the centreline of the body

Excerpts were taken from

Wikapedia

'The Root of Chinese Qigong' by Dr Yang Jwing-Ming

The Shaolin Jee Shin Wing Chun Kung Fu web site

www.shaolinjeeshinwingchun.com.au

Yip man legendary Grand Master of Wing Chun

Linda with David Cheung on
Linda's graduation day in December 1994

Qigong master
Dr Shan Hui Xu 1995

Linda with Grandmaster William Cheung on his birthday 2005.

Presenting a koala on my first meeting with
Grandmaster Fung Chun at Dr Leung Jan's House, Kulo village China
November 2006

Garry, Myself and Grandmaster Fung Chun at his house
in Kulo Village 2007

Sifu Fung Keun, Garry and myself in Sifu Donald Macs
training hall, Kowloon/ Hong Kong, after a week of private tuition with, Sifu
Fung Keun, son of Grandmaster Fung Chun December 2008.

Garry and myself with Australian born International martial artist and movie
star Richard Norton 2011. Richard presented Garry and I with our Sports
Development and Sports Coaching Diplomas.

Index

Notes

Concepts, Principles and Golden rules